LIFE

at the Lakes

STORIES TO IMPROVE FINANCIAL WELLNESS

ROD RIEU CFP® FCSI

One Printers Way
Altona, MB R0G 0B0,
Canada

www.friesenpress.com

First Edition — 2021

The information in this book is presented as general reference material only. The author and the publisher are not in this book offering or providing legal, tax, investment, insurance, financial, accounting, or other professional advice or services. The ideas, methods, plans, suggestions and other information in this book may not be appropriate for all individuals and are not put forward as being appropriate for any particular individual or circumstance. No one should use or apply the information in this book in particular circumstances without advice from a competent professional informed by thorough consideration of such circumstances. Examples discussed in this book are illustrative only; the author and publisher do not warrant or guarantee any results or outcomes.

The ideas and views expressed in this book are the author's alone. No other person or entity, including the author's employer, has reviewed, endorsed or approved the contents of this book. All of the author's efforts in connection with this book were and are outside the scope of his employment.

The author, publisher and their agents assume no responsibility for errors or omissions. They expressly disclaim all liability, loss or risk, personal or otherwise, that results or may result, directly or indirectly, from the use or application of any information in this book.

For information about special discounts for bulk purchases, please contact Rod Rieu at lifeatthelakes.rodrieu@gmail.com

ISBN
978-1-03-910730-4 (Hardcover)
978-1-03-910729-8 (Paperback)
978-1-03-910731-1 (eBook)

Business & Economics, Personal Finance, Money Management

Distributed to the trade by The Ingram Book Company

For Nathan and Emily,
you are my compass.

Jill

my long term friend

all my best

Ned Rein

Table of Contents

CHAPTER 1

Financial Freedom

As I lifted the cold Heineken up to my lips, I saw Ed, the bartender, talking to a couple down at the end of the bar. The woman's piercing green eyes looked deeply at the man she was with, and his arm draped over her shoulder with the confidence of a man in love. Watching Ed talk to the couple reminded me of how I had screwed up my life.

Ed glanced over to me; he must have seen the sadness in my eyes. He shook the couple's hands and as he poured them each a glass of champagne, he waved his hand as if to say *this is on the house.* Ed walked over as he cracked open another beer for me.

"Thanks Ed," I said, putting the empty Heineken down. "Who are those folks?"

"Newlyweds, here on their honeymoon," he said with a smile.

"Poor sap. Might be cheaper for him to write her a cheque now for $25,000 and call it a day," I replied bitterly.

Ed shook his head and chuckled. "Not everyone screws up relationships like you, my friend."

"You know, you are an S.O.B.," I laughed.

Ed laughed as he started to pour a glass of Zinfandel for the server waiting at the bar.

"How many alimony cheques are you writing again every month?" he mocked me.

"Still paying two," I replied with a sigh.

Ed smiled at me, lifting my spirits as only a good friend can as he mixed another drink. "You have fared pretty good financially, despite being divorced twice. Why the long face? You have a good job running the wealth management arm of Mainland Financial, live in a nice townhouse in beautiful Kelowna, and get to come here, to the Dancing Otter, and talk to me." He laughed.

"My years of training as a financial planner in Vancouver, with dreams of living in the million-dollar home and driving the silver Porsche with millions in the bank, have been shattered by my inability to maintain a decent relationship," I said bluntly.

"You sure know a lot about money, Cal," Ed said seriously, "but I don't think you really know much about financial freedom."

My eyes widened as I looked at him. "What are you talking about?" My tone felt a little too harsh.

"I think you need to revisit your values, my friend," he said with compassionate eyes and a caring smile. "You are one of the dumbest smart guys I know."

I couldn't help but laugh at Ed's mocking. "All right, I'm out of here," I said, pushing away my half-full bottle of Heineken. Standing up, putting on my black overcoat that all guys in suits seem to wear, I glanced over at the happy newlyweds, who were laughing and clearly in love. I turned to the door and began walking out. Bitterness, it seemed, could not be cured by alcohol.

As I walked down Brian Avenue towards Keith Street, heading home, my phone buzzed. I looked down and saw I had received a text from my sister, Nadia.

Whatcha doin'? read the text.

Just walking back home from the Otter, I replied to my only sister.

It's nice that you can walk to the bar. Brent, myself, and the kids are going to come by for the July long weekend. Your nephews want to see their uncle this summer.

The boys loved coming to my townhouse because they got to stay in the third bedroom by themselves with their own TV to play their Nintendo. Brent and Nadia also knew most of my six other neighbours and enjoyed the picnics in the courtyard. Each of the seven units brought some food and we had a couple drinks and a great time.

You bet, you are always welcome. I replied. A smile came across my face as I thought about how lucky I was to have such a great and supportive family.

As I turned onto Keith and entered the gate of the complex, I noticed Jessica Walters watering the flowers. Jessica has lived at the Lakes for several years with her husband Henry. At seventy years old, she was slender and always well dressed. As the unofficial greeter of the Lakes, Jessica kept fit by maintaining the beautiful juniper bushes and rose garden as well as the three other gardens at the Lakes.

"Hi Calvin," she chimed.

"Hi Jessica. The flowers look beautiful as usual. How is Henry?" I asked, stopping to glance at the flowers.

"Oh, he is grumpy as always," she replied.

I enjoyed talking and having a beer with Henry on the deck. Not only did Henry enjoy having a beer, he was also a connoisseur of good scotch. His years at the mill had taken a toll on him, making him that good kind of grumpy that some older guys are that always makes you smile. At seventy-one years old, Henry was trying to enjoy his retirement, but the past ten years of worrying about how to maintain his lifestyle was wearing on him. Jessica, on the other hand, was content gardening and spending time with her grandchildren.

"Calvin, maybe you can talk to Henry and help him with the money thing. I swear that man is never content." Jessica sighed as she removed some petals from the rose bush.

Over the several beers that Henry and I have shared, he has never been able to understand why Jessica left the entire financial burden to him.

"I will pop over later to see Henry and have a chat on the deck. Also, in order to help Henry relax, I will bring the beer."

Jessica's laugh rang out and brought a smile to my face. She had such contentment—she was a breath of fresh air.

I slid my key into unit three and entered my three-bedroom townhouse. As I entered the foyer, I turned left into the kitchen. With stainless-steel appliances, a marble dining room set, a dual sink, and built-in vacuum system, it was a nice place, at least for one person. After being married twice, having my own place was both peaceful and lonesome. I hadn't reached my financial freedom goals and felt like both a fraud and financial expert at the same time.

The fact that I still had a mortgage on this place was depressing, but I needed to remember that with all of the money I had paid out in legal fees and divorce settlements (approaching seven figures!), my financial planning background and training had served me well. Sometimes, especially given my education and background, I felt like a failure. Financial freedom, it seemed, had eluded me. As it turns out, they don't teach interpersonal relationships in business school. Maybe I should have taken courses in that instead.

I looked over at the picture of my dad on the fireplace mantle. I remembered having the first taste of financial freedom when I was twelve years old. I would get on my little purple three-speed bike and pedal to McLean Park to bat boy for the regular baseball tournaments. My dad was the manager of the Commercial Hotel Bears and my uncles played for the Arms Pub. Growing up on the baseball field with all of these people from different walks of life playing ball, drinking beer and cheering on their friends was a memory I would cherish for my whole life.

Every time I would bat boy, I would earn fifty cents. After I did three games, I had enough money to buy a delicious grease-laden hamburger with fried onions cooked by the volunteers, who were wives and girlfriends of players, coaches, and spectators. The smell of grease and fried onions was still, to this day, a great memory that reminded me of that taste of freedom. Earning money to purchase my own food was an early lesson in financial freedom.

I pulled the door of the fridge open and grabbed a diet cola as I wandered over to the living room. I sat down on the recliner, turned on the TV. Entering the seventh inning, Vladimir Guerrero Jr and the Toronto Blue Jays were trailing the Yankees 4-3. It made me reminisce about the trip my friend Shane and I took to the East Coast. It was September and the baseball season was winding down. This trip was something I dreamt about for a long time. As we flew into Boston on that Sunday, prior to going to see the Jays lose to the Red Sox, I was excited about taking a tour of Fenway Park. Feeling the nostalgia and thinking about the things that had happened in that historical ballpark was amazing. The tour guide, Pete, took us onto the field where the Red Sox were warming up. We had to stay behind the rope, but being on the field at Fenway was a dream come true. Definitely the highlight of the trip was when Pete took Shane and I up to sit on the Green Monster. This large wall in left field was iconic and there we were—sitting on top. Shane and I took out our Sharpies and signed the foul pole. We knew they would paint over it, but under that paint would be our signatures forever. We were in the place that housed Yastrzemski, Clemens, Boggs and once upon a time Ruth. That trip that took us to Citi Field to see the Mets beat the Marlins, and then over to Yankee Stadium to watch the Yankees beat my beloved Jays will forever live in my memory. We ended our trip driving to Philadelphia to watch the

Phillies play the Marlins before finishing in Baltimore, finally seeing the Jays win. A smile crossed my face as I thought of the fun Shane and I had on that trip—a trip of a lifetime. While I certainly love baseball and going to these "cathedrals," it was having my good friend there that made the trip so special. I started to realize that financial freedom in itself is not about the money, but what you do with the money and who you do it with.

Being single had its advantages, as I did have a fair bit of money in the bank along with my Registered Retirement Savings Plans (commonly known as an RRSP), Tax-Free Savings Account (which I had invested in stocks), and excellent pension plan. Being in wealth management working for Mainland had its benefits; they paid me well and I got to work with a team of excellent financial advisors and assist the staff that worked in our twenty-five branches to help customers with their financial problems and goals.

I looked over at the statue of *The Thinker* that I had picked up in Rome. I wondered what he was actually thinking. It made me think about the trip I took by myself to Italy and France and the importance of getting to know yourself.

I decided to take the trip last fall; I needed to go somewhere to clear my head. One of my lifelong goals was to go to the Louvre and also see some art at the Vatican Museums and the statues in Florence. One thing that I had actually never done was truly be alone. While seeing this art and architecture was important, getting to know myself was the main goal.

I flew into Rome, where I sat on cobblestone patios drinking wine and eating the best carbonara I have ever had. After spending three days in Rome, I then flew to Florence and spent the next six days in Tuscany. The highlight was renting a villa in a thousand-year-old village in Chianti and having dinner and wine with Christian and Eva. Christian was a chef and brought me into his home and taught me how to make carbonara while we drank some terrific Tuscan Chianti and shared stories about life in Tuscany . . . and love. My trip ended with six days in Paris, where I was able to climb the Eiffel Tower and see the *Mona Lisa* in the Louvre.

Reminiscing on all of this made me realize that I was lucky enough to have ticked several boxes off of my bucket list. Most of all, I thought about how lucky I was to have the means to spend time just with myself, having good friends that I could travel with or being comfortable to meet new friends. Maybe Ed was right; maybe I needed to rethink my values. After all I am not hurting for money. I opened the door to the fridge and pulled out a couple beers. It would be nice to go have a chat with Henry.

Key Learnings:

- What does financial freedom mean to me?
- Relationships can have a big impact on financial freedom
- At one time in my life, $1.50 represented financial freedom

CHAPTER 2

The Calvin Bennett Method

I wandered next door to unit four and rapped on the door. A tall thin man with a grey beard answered the door.

"Hi Henry," I said with a smile. "Have beer, will travel."

Henry's grin went from ear to ear as he took a beer out of my hand and motioned for me to sit. We sat on his beige chairs on the patio at the front of his unit. The freshly trimmed rose bushes looked beautiful; Jessica had done a great job.

"How are things, Henry?" I inquired.

"The COVID-19 pandemic was tough on my portfolio," Henry replied. "I lost some money when I had to sell to take some income."

The pandemic of 2020 was devastating for many people. Even though the cardinal rule to investing was buy low, sell high, many people sold at the bottom. In fact, in March of 2020, there was a record for people selling: almost double the second-highest negative fund flow in history. Even though 2020 did well in the markets, many people lost thousands, while those that waded in when the market fell did well.

"I love my wife, Calvin, but she just doesn't understand the stress this volatility causes me. How do I deal with these losses in my portfolio and provide for my wife? She is concerned about leaving money for the kids and grandchildren, but if we don't manage things, there will be nothing left. My investments are in a low-risk balanced mutual fund, so I should be protected. I need the income from my investments every month to live so when the market goes down, I end up being forced to sell every month to generate the income. When I sell my mutual fund when the market was down, it really affects my portfolio, and I end up losing money. I wish I didn't have to sell, but we need the money."

I knew what Henry was talking about. He was dealing with one of my financial advisors, one of our younger advisors. This particular advisor, Domenic, had the goal of running a clean, simple practice. By putting people into balanced funds, he didn't have to do much money management because the fund manager does all of the buying, selling, and rebalancing. After all, it was the fund manager and all of their analysts that are studying the companies and following the markets. It does make sense to let the experts do this work. However, for those needing an income, it can become stressful when the market falls and they are required to sell every month.

I know that Henry and Jessica converted their RRSP into a Registered Retirement Income Fund, or RRIF, to generate income. I also know that they have taken advantage of Tax-Free Savings Accounts as well. TFSAs are an excellent way for the average person to save for retirement.

"Tell me about how your investments are set up, Henry, and what you are looking to achieve." I took a sip of beer.

"Well," said Henry, "I have about $500,000 split between both of our RRIF and TFSAs. We need $1,000 per month to supplement our income and we take out $10,000 per year to travel. I really wish I didn't have to because I have to pay tax on the RRIFs. I wish I never bought those damn things. Every time I withdraw $10,000, the bank holds 20% for income tax, and I still owe money at the end of the year. I trust Domenic, and I know you work with him, but he just keeps saying long term, stay for the long term. The mutual fund I have is good, and I know the advice is good, but I am not sure what to do. Jessica, bless her heart, just told me to stop worrying, it will all work out, we need to enjoy our life and stop worrying so much. I am the one who handles the investments and she just doesn't understand the long-term implications of this. While I get that I am okay, this money will disappear and there will be less for the kids or grandkids, not to mention what will happen if one of us has to go to a long-term care facility or we have other medical expenses. This money is important to us and our family's future. Also, we are hoping to leave some money to the church. They have been such a great community for us, and they do such great work. Domenic is great, but he keeps running retirement scenarios and said as long as I stay the course, I will be fine. I admit that I am glad I listened to him through the pandemic, but he just doesn't understand my concerns. Maybe it's because he is so young, I don't know."

Henry, like many older adults I knew, was rightfully frustrated. He listened to the pundits in the '90s and maximized his RRSPs for himself and Jessica, thinking he needed a million dollars to retire. He was finding out that the tax benefits he received in the '90s were coming back to roost in his retirement. It is so important to have proper retirement planning. Things like how much income you will need at retirement, and what you estimate your tax levels to be are important considerations. It is very tempting to pack away all of your money into an RRSP and get that immediate gratification of the tax refund. Thirty or forty percent of our contributions is a nice amount to get back at the end of the year. Theoretically, it is great because you can reinvest that into your TFSA or pay down your mortgage with that refund, but like a lot of things, theory and reality can be two different things.

Henry and Jessica, like a lot of Canadians, used that money as "found" money and spent it frivolously, buying things they didn't need and essentially blowing it. They were now realizing that they owe that money back to the government because they have to pay tax on their withdrawals. For most Canadians, a balanced approach to TFSAs and RRSPs is a good strategy. Resisting the temptation of that instant tax refund will give you peace of mind in retirement. When you withdraw money from your TFSA, because it is tax-free, you are getting one-hundred-cent dollars, whereas withdrawing from your RRSP, because you have to pay tax on it, will only give you sixty- to eighty-cent dollars and, god forbid, if you pass away with money in the RRSP and your kids get it, they may end up with fifty-cent dollars.

While your basic math and theory will tell you that the RRSP and TFSA are the same at retirement, the big difference is the human difference. We can do all the math in the world, but spending money and living a life is where the human element comes in. Saving taxes twenty-five years ago is not a lot of comfort to older adults living on a fixed income today. It is how we use the money in retirement that matters. There is peace of mind that comes with one-hundred-cent dollars verses fifty-cent dollars.

"Calvin," said Henry, "I am not sure what to do here. Jessica wants to help the kids and we both want to help the church, but I am concerned about running out of money."

"Henry," I said, "this discussion is less about what you do with your money and more about what financial freedom means to you. It doesn't matter what you do with your money. You will still be worried when the market goes down, you will still worry about leaving money to the kids and church, and you will always worry about running out of money."

I can see on Henry's face as he glanced up, looking at the beautiful cloudless night, that he was concerned.

"Financial freedom is different for both Jessica and me. Jessica wants to live day to day and not worry about the money, as long as there was some left over for the kids and church. I am more detail-oriented and want some concrete answers," Henry said as he furrowed his brow and rubbed his forehead in obvious frustration.

Henry's frustration comes because we live in an investment world that deals in future promise versus promises today. Understanding what financial freedom meant was just that: freedom.

Henry was financially strong; however, he was not free. He was worried and concerned about making the right choice, selling low, and paying taxes. We agreed that in order to help him enjoy his retirement life, he needed more certainty in his income and comfort that there would be something left for the kids.

Henry flicked the porch light on as we chatted. First of all, we decided on the income. We agreed that it made sense to pull the $1,000 per month out of the RRIF. With $250,000 in the RRIF, we would need to take out just about 5% per year. We actually needed a little more than that to satisfy government minimum withdrawal amounts. We knew that getting 2.5% on a term deposit would not make Henry feel good, so we needed to set up a system.

I got up from my chair at the front of his house and said, "I am going to tell you about the Calvin Bennett method while I get a couple more cold beers."

Henry's face lit up in a smile. He was anxious to hear about the Calvin Bennett method. As I came back from my place with two more cold beers in my hand, I reflected on the differences in freedom that Jessica and Henry had. While Henry had a lot of money and was controlling it, his stress and anxiety around the money was more like financial jail than financial freedom.

"Okay, Henry, here is what we are going to do," I said as I cracked open the beers. "First of all, we will put $12,000 of your RRIF into a high interest savings account. This account doesn't pay well, but there is zero fluctuation and we will draw your income out of this. We will take another $113,000 and ladder it in GICs and bonds. What I mean by this is that we will break it up into ten pieces of $11,300 each. These will each pay out between 2-4%."

Henry sipped his beer, nodding along with me.

"So, each bond or GIC will pay out between $226 and $452 per year in interest for a total of about $4,000 per year. This will now give you eleven years of income. You will not have to sell low because they are bonds and GICs and, even though the bonds will have some volatility, you will hold them to maturity. Each year a term deposit or bond will mature and the interest on the bonds and GICs will pay into your high interest savings account, building that up. Each year an $11,300 GIC or bond will pay out, giving you the income you need for the next year. Still with me?" My beer was slowly warming in my hand, so I set it down on the small table in front of me. "Also, with the interest paying out, you will have enough money available every month to give you your income."

Henry cleared his throat. "What do we do with the rest of the money?"

I nodded. "Good question! The balance will go into equity mutual funds. Equity funds are mostly invested in companies or stocks. This will fluctuate like crazy, but will accomplish what your balance funds accomplish, a split between equities and fixed income. Now, you will want to meet with our advisor Domenic every year to rebalance so that you always have at least five years of income in cash, bonds and term deposits."

The streetlights were slowly flicking on as I continued. "The beauty of the Calvin Bennett method is that if one year you are in, say, a pandemic, you will not need to sell, since you have lots of time to wait for a recovery. By setting the dividends or distributions of the mutual fund to pay out into your high interest savings account, you are able to maintain income for a longer period of time. When you meet annually, if the market is up, sell some of your mutual funds and buy more longer-term bonds and term deposits to keep that ladder going. If you can average 2% in distributions, the rest of the growth will allow you to get your $1,000 per month well into your nineties."

I picked up a napkin and wrote an example of the Calvin Bennett method on the back:

RRIF Total: $ 250,000

High Interest Savings Account: $ 12,000. Take $ 1,000 per month for income. This will automatically pay into your chequing account.

$ 11,300 – 1-year GIC
$ 11,300 – 2-year GIC
$ 11,300 – 3-year GIC
$ 11,300 – 4-year GIC
$ 11,300 – 5-year GIC
$ 11,300 – 6-year Government Bond
$ 11,300 – 7-year Government Bond
$ 11,300 – 8-year Government Bond
$ 11,300 – 9-year Government Bond
$ 11,300 – 10-year Government Bond
$ 125,000 – Equity Mutual Funds

"After the end of the first year, you will have depleted the $12,000 high interest savings account because you are taking $1,000 per month out. This will be replenished by the roughly $4,000 in interest that was paid out, along with the maturing one-year GIC that will pay out into your high interest savings account, for a total of just over $17,000. This will be enough plus a little extra for the next twelve months. Your two-year GIC will have one year left and will mature into your high interest savings account, along with the interest payments to pay your income requirement for the following year."

Henry scrutinized the napkin.

I leaned in. "Meet with your advisor and decide, if the market is up, if you should sell $11,300 and purchase another ten-year bond. If it is a good time, then sell it, if not, wait until there is a good time. After all, you truly will have a long-term investment, with at least eleven years until your laddered investments run out."

"So," said Henry, tapping the napkin in his hand, "what you are saying, Calvin, is that I have better control of when I sell the equities and I can have GICs and bonds maturing every year over the next ten years. That, along with the interest and dividends, will pay my income for at least ten years, probably more?"

He squinted into the darkening yard. "I should sell the equities when the time is right and then I don't have to sell every month? I can sell when it is beneficial for me to do so, as long as it is an up year? I don't have to sell every year?"

He nodded, as if to himself. "Okay, that sounds like something that will help me with my anxiety about the markets every month and able to get my income monthly. But we still haven't talked about travelling every year, leaving money for the kids, money for the church or all of the taxes that I will have to pay."

I could see now that I had some more work to do with Henry, so we switched over to drinks with more potency—Jessica's coffee. Jessica Walters was known for three things at the Lakes: her niceness, how good she was at taking care of the gardens, and how strong her coffee was. Jessica poured us some coffee as Henry explained the Calvin Bennett method of retirement income to her.

"Calvin is now going to show us how we can travel as well as ensure the kids and the church are taken care of."

Jessica poured herself a cup of coffee and joined us.

"Tell me about the travel you want to do," I said.

Jessica chimed in. "Well, ideally, we want to go to Arizona every year for a couple of months. We find that it costs us an extra $6,000 per year to go there. But we also want to take the kids and grandkids on a vacation every five years or so. It's high-quality time for us and we really want to enjoy our time with them. We love spending time with them, and this vacation time is so wonderful. We absolutely adore our grandchildren and they are so busy that we don't get enough quality time with them."

I realized quickly that spending quality time with her family was one of Jessica's definitions of financial freedom. The ability to, without bitterness or putting the kids in a tough spot, spend two solid weeks with her children and grandchildren would make her life so much better. An added bonus was the ability to plan for the vacation. After all, planning for a vacation is part of the enjoyment and brings the families together. Having something to look forward to is so important. My experience of not having something to look forward to, like a vacation or spending time with a friend, taught me the value of relationships, hope and promise. Just waiting for everything to reopen after the pandemic and looking forward to the ability to travel again was painful. But when I was able to plan another trip and have something to look forward to, my mental health was so much better.

"Okay," I said. "Let's apply the Calvin Bennett method to your vacations. First of all, we know that you have $250,000 in your TFSA and regular investment accounts. Where would you like to take the kids and grandkids?"

"Well, it would be great to go to Disney for a week," Henry replied. I could see by his enthusiasm that spending time with the grandkids and seeing a smile on their faces was also an important value of his. It turns out that there was more to life than safety and security for Henry: part of financial freedom to him was spending time with his family.

"How much do you want to spend on them for this trip?" I asked.

"Well, I figure $20,000 will get us all down to California, set us up in hotels for the week and get us into Disneyland. I am sure the kids can fund the rest." Henry explained this with a big smile on his face. He had clearly spent some time thinking about this and planning it. I didn't think I had ever seen the grin on Henry's face so big.

"Okay, Henry, what have you learned about the Calvin Bennett method? How can we make this happen?"

"Laddering term deposits?" asked Henry.

"Yes, sort of," I replied. "This money is your emergency money, extra money and travel money. Some is taxable, some is tax free. The good news is that it is not an RRSP, so we are dealing with one-hundred-cent dollars. First of all, with your $250,000, you have $150,000 in non-registered money and $100,000 in your Tax-Free Savings Accounts."

Back when Henry was working for the mill in New Westminster and Jessica was working at the dentist office, they bought a home there. When they bought it, it was in a nice area, and like many people, they updated and remodelled it every year. Their choice to sell their home and buy at the Lakes allowed them to pay cash for their townhouse, maximize their TFSAs, and put more money into the bank. For many living in the lower mainland of British Columbia, this became a good strategy to help fund retirement.

"We will need to put the first $20,000 in an emergency fund that is accessible. This will pay low interest, but it is accessible in the event of a financial emergency. Because the interest is low, we will have it in your regular or 'open' money, as we call it in the investment business. Next, we need a further $26,000 in a short-term account. This will be your trip money next year to Disneyland, as well as your Arizona money. This takes care of the first $46,000. Next, we will buy a five-year GIC for $26,000 and a ten-year bond for $26,000. These, along with the interest they generate, will help pay for the next two trips. Because the interest will be a little higher and the interest is 100% taxable, we will put them in your Tax-Free Savings Account. We will now put in GICs and bonds for one to four years and six to nine years each for $6,000. These along with the interest will help get you to Arizona for the next ten years. We will split these up between your TFSA and your open accounts. This takes care of $146,000."

I flipped over the napkin and wrote this strategy on the other side.

$20,000 Savings Account – Emergency
$26,000 Savings Account – Disney next year
$6,000 One-year term deposit – Arizona
$6,000 Two-year term deposit – Arizona
$6,000 Three-year term deposit – Arizona
$6,000 Four-year term deposit – Arizona
$26,000 Five-year term deposit – Family trip
$6,000 Six-year bond – Arizona
$6,000 Seven-year bond – Arizona
$6,000 Eight-year bond – Arizona
$6,000 Nine-year bond – Arizona
$26,000 Ten-year bond – Trip

$146,000 = Total

"There you go!" I passed the napkin to Jessica. "We have just funded your next ten trips, all with little market fluctuation and with minimized tax. The interest will help pay for the effects that inflation will have on your trips. This leaves you with about $104,000. Let's talk about the church. How about we leave money for the kids and the church and try and keep income taxes to the CRA to a minimum?" Now, I have had many beers with Henry and knew that nothing boiled his blood more than paying taxes to CRA. "Tell me, Henry, how do you feel about life insurance?"

Henry looked over to Jessica in disbelief. "Okay, Calvin, so far what you are saying makes sense. However, life insurance is for protection, and I am seventy-one years old. Do you know how expensive that is?"

Over the years, I have learned there are many uses for life insurance, but there is one universal truth: life insurance is for protection when someone dies. It is great for young families, to give them peace of mind in the event that something happens to one of the parents, but people often fail to see the benefit of providing tax-free dollars upon death and let the insurance company pay for costs—like taxes.

"Okay, Henry, let's make an assumption. Let's say that you and Jessica pass away in twenty years. Let's also assume that you have $50,000 in taxable RRIFs left. Here is what will happen with that money. Historically, in marriages, about 85% of the time, the man dies first. There are a few reasons for that. First of all, women tend to outlive men, and generally speaking, men in many marriages are older. There are lots of exceptions, but those are generalizations. So, chances are, Henry, you will die first and then Jessica will pass away. When you die, your RRIF, because you have named her as beneficiary, will roll over to Jessica into her name, tax free. It is when she dies and there is no spouse to roll it over to that the RRIF will become taxable. Depending on her income and any other taxable income sources she may have in her year of death, this would likely push her into a fifty-percent tax bracket, causing her to pay half of her RRIF money in tax."

Henry's eyes widened and his eyebrows furrowed. "We would pay 50%?"

"The more income you earn in a year, the more tax you pay. In the year of death, the CRA deems that your assets are sold and cashed in, including your RRIF. This means that Jessica's income will be very high in her year of death and likely push her into the higher tax bracket," I replied as I took a sip of my coffee.

Jessica put her hand on Henry's arm. "Is there anything we can do about that?" she asked.

I shifted in my seat. "Yes, there is. Here is what I suggest we do. We will put $20,000 into a joint and last-to-die prescribed annuity that will pay out an income as long as one of you is still alive. Because of your age and the fact that prescribed annuities pay out principal and interest, the income attracts very little tax. We will use this money to fund a joint and last-to-die insurance policy. This policy will pay out $50,000 when the second person dies, providing $50,000 tax free upon the second person's death. It doesn't matter who passes first, or when they pass, it will pay out on the second person's death."

"I don't like the sound of that. Why would we want to pay out money on our death, who would it go to?" Jessica sounded worried.

"This money would go to the church as a donation in the year of your death. So, what would normally happen is at the death of the surviving person, she would take $50,000 into income from the remaining RRIF on their death, pay $25,000 to CRA, and the other $25,000 would go to her kids. Essentially, this makes your kids and the CRA joint beneficiaries of your RRIF. Instead, in this case, the $50,000 would pay out to the church as a donation. This donation would offset the RRIF income, so the church gets $50,000, the kids get your $50,000 RRIF tax free, and the CRA would get nothing."

I saw Jessica's eyes light up as her concerns about the church and ensuring her kids get some money were addressed. I then saw Henry's eyebrows furrow. "What if we live longer and there are no taxes to pay on the RRIF because we cashed it in?" he asked.

"Well, that will fund the Calvin Bennett beer fund—I will have $50,000 for beer for life!" We all laughed.

"I am just kidding," I said with a smile. "The $50,000 would still pay out. It could pay out to the church, or you could change the beneficiary so that some of the money could go to the kids, grandchildren or anyone else that you want to see the money go to. All you would need to do is change the beneficiary. It is very simple and gives you full control of who the money ends up going to. You want to make sure you speak to a qualified insurance specialist to ensure it is set up correctly." I once again pulled out another napkin and wrote on the back.

<u>Do nothing</u>
RRIF $ 50,000
CRA $ 25,000
Beneficiary $ 25,000
Church $ 0
Total to Beneficiaries and Church: $ 25,000

<u>Spend $ 20,000 on Annuity/Life Insurance</u>
RRIF $ 50,000
Church $ 50,000
Beneficiary $ 50,000
CRA $ 0
Total Beneficiaries and Church $ 100,000

Showing the napkin to them, I said, "For the $20,000 annuity and a little bit of estate planning, the amount that you would pass on to your beneficiaries and to the church goes from $25,000 to $100,000."

I passed this napkin to Henry. "That takes care of another $20,000 and leaves us with $84,000. With the balance, we finish off the Calvin Bennett method. We put that money into equities, maximizing your TFSA first, and then the balance into your open account. With this, you can replenish your emergency fund or ladder another bond when the market is up, again giving you control of when you are selling your equities. This can then be truly a longer-term investment."

Jessica gave me a wink and a smile as we could see the weight of the financial world come off Henry's shoulders.

"But we haven't talked about returns," Henry said.

"Henry," I said, leaning in. "One of the illusions in the financial world is that we think we have control over our returns by timing the markets. If this were true, we would have money managers running around with 25% annual track records. Timing the market and knowing the exact time to buy or sell is a myth. Realistically, we can expect 6-7% in equities over the long term, provided you don't sell out at the wrong time. So, in the case of our $250,000 RRIF, we have it invested 50% fixed income and 50% equities. Assuming 6% on $125,000 of equities and 3% on $125,000 of fixed income, we would see about $11,250 in returns on average."

Henry nodded along, encouraging me to keep talking.

"Unfortunately, there is nothing average about equities. Therefore, many people want control over their returns, so they invest in just fixed income. You can do that at 3% and earn $7,500 per year. But this would cost you about $3,750, just over $300 per month in lost returns over the long term. Put another way, it works out to 30% of your $1,000 monthly income. While we want the best returns possible, allocating your assets properly will ensure you get a good return. By using the Calvin Bennett method and an advisor to help you stay the course, you give up mythical control of returns but get peace of mind and get closer to your goal of financial freedom."

Jessica brought out some cookies for us to share. Homemade peanut butter cookies have been part of the reason I have a few too many pounds on me. That and the beer.

"This is a great plan, Calvin," Jessica said. "But what if one of us has to go into a care facility? We have looked after the kids and the church, paid for our lifestyle and travel, and kept taxes down, but what if something doesn't go to plan?"

I took a sip of my coffee and grabbed another one of Jessica's delicious peanut butter cookies. As a financial planner for many years, there seemed to be a universal truth. Men seemed to be more concerned about how much money they were making and keeping fees down, while women were more concerned about ensuring the money grew enough and was safe enough so that their family was taken care of. Presenting solutions to men and women was often different as they usually had different definitions of financial freedom. For financial advisors, keeping that in mind can help them help their clients understand each other better and help them reach their goals.

"Jessica, that is a real possibility. Some people purchase long-term care insurance or critical illness insurance, which are good options. In your case, it will come down to choices. If it happened while you both are alive and within the next ten years, you will likely need to revisit your travel plans."

Jessica reached for Henry's hand.

"People often forget that their home is also an investment," I reminded them gently. "There are three solutions to pay for long-term care in your situation. First is a reverse mortgage. Theoretically, it is a good option because you can access the equity in your home, let's say up to 55%, in either a lump sum or monthly payments. You don't have to pay it back until you choose to move or pass away. This would allow you to stay in your home while paying for these care options. In reality, your personal definition of financial freedom will be tested because you will be taking on debt and many people have a hard time taking on debt in their seventies and eighties. Are you following me so far?"

Henry and Jessica both nodded, still holding hands.

"The second option is a home equity line of credit. This would allow you to access the equity in your home, but you would be required to pay the interest. The interest costs will likely be less, but those costs could impact your cash flow. Remember, if one of you has to go to a care home, it is likely that your home expenses will become less as the care expenses rise. The other option is to sell your home and rent or move in with the kids. The money from the home can help pay for the care facility as well as draw an income for rent. For example, your house is worth $400,000. Simply put, the $400,000 could provide you with income for several years. By putting someone you trust as Power of Attorney, like your kids, they can help get you to get set up so that you can access the equity in your home either by selling it or accessing a home equity line of credit. Of course, if one of you passes away and the survivor goes into a care facility, the power of attorney will come in very handy as the attorney will be able to take care of the financial arrangements such as rebalancing investments, ensuring there is cash flow available to fund health care, managing daily living expenses or larger expenses, and selling assets such as the house."

Both Jessica and Henry looked a little uncomfortable with this topic of conversation, so I tried to sound reassuring as I continued. "I know it's not easy to talk about. May I keep going?"

They both nodded. "If one of you has passed away and the other is in long-term care, selling the house is a good option to ensure you are taken care of. While it would be great to plan on leaving the house to the beneficiaries, having it as another emergency fund for care expenses will free up some of your money to do things like spend more time in Arizona, take your family to Disneyland, or just cover your day-to-day expenses. More importantly, it allows you to focus on what is important in your life. Money is an enabler, enabling you to live the life you want."

Both Jessica and Henry were deep in thought, and I could see the wheels turning in their heads thinking about planning their time with their families in Disneyland and how they were going to approach Domenic about setting up their financial plans differently to ensure both of their visions of financial freedom were realized.

It was getting late, so I thanked Jessica and Henry for the coffee and cookies as I started walking across the courtyard back to my unit. Financial freedom seemed to be less about how much money they had, but what the money could do for them. For Jessica, it was about spending time with her family, ensuring she and Henry would be okay and making a positive difference in the lives of her family and church. For Henry, it was about peace of mind. He wanted to ensure that Jessica's dreams came true, while not worrying about interest rates, stock markets, and volatility. I found out that night how much effort Henry put into loving his wife and ensuring she was provided for. Henry and Jessica loved spending their time with each other and their families. Henry loved his wife and that was what made up the definition of financial freedom for him. Hopefully Henry's mind was eased.

It seemed for Henry and Jessica that financial freedom was not about how much money they had. Financial freedom, for them, was all about love.

Key Learnings:

- Draw income out of low volatility investments
- Using Bond and Term Deposit Ladders can give you peace of mind in your RRIF
- Rebalance your investments on a regular basis—buy low, sell high
- Use non-conventional means like insurance to reduce RRIF Taxes
- Discuss what Financial Freedom means with your spouse

CHAPTER 3

Taking Care of the Important Things

"Can you please babysit for us tomorrow night?" Kaylin Williamson was pleading with me.

Their babysitter had cancelled on them on their fifth wedding anniversary. The winery that they had their dinner plans at had a world-renowned chef who had moved to the beautiful Okanagan to come back to her roots and live out her passion in our majestic countryside.

I remember when Kaylin and Nathan brought home Justin, their first child, three years ago, when Kaylin was twenty-four and Nathan was twenty-three. Just three months ago, young Taylor had arrived. Justin was a spark of a young boy who was very curious about the world, and Taylor was a beautiful baby girl. I can see how tired Nathan is; working as a lawyer at Robinson and Reid kept Nathan working long days and nights and the kids kept him busy at home.

I remember when I was married and the kids were young. Often, I would go to work and the kids were in bed, and when I got home from work, the kids were in bed. I would imagine that for Nathan, spending time alone with Kaylin was a rare opportunity.

Working in the financial world, I had been to many Chamber of Commerce events that Nathan attended as well. I was pleased when I ran into Nathan at events. I could see how well-respected he was amongst his peers and the business community. He had a terrific future ahead of him, and, for that matter, so did Kaylin.

The office of Kaylin's massage therapy practice has a beautiful view overlooking a lavender farm. I once went to see Kaylin at her office and walked through the lavender farm before my session. The beauty and the aroma were a wonderful way to begin relaxing prior to my session. Savannah Logan, who used to run the business before Kaylin took over, came out of retirement to run the practice while Kaylin was on maternity leave. She shared office space with a chiropractor and physiotherapist.

I knew Kaylin was a little concerned about going back to work in about six months. Being self-employed didn't allow her to benefit from the government programs that allowed regularly employed people to share some maternity and paternity benefits with their spouses.

I had never met two harder-working people than Kaylin and Nathan. When they were not working, they were cooking, cleaning, and taking care of the kids, giving them baths, feeding them, and changing their dirty diapers. As much as I love kids, changing diapers was something I had not missed. They say that there is a huge difference in changing your child's diapers versus somebody else's child. Your own kid's diapers don't smell as bad, apparently. I didn't like changing my own children's diapers, and it looked like tomorrow night I would be changing other kids' diapers after all.

"No problem, Kaylin," I replied. "You will love your dinner at Lakeside, their new chef is absolutely amazing."

A smile grew across Nathan's face. He had a glint in his eye and a mischievous smile, I could tell he was looking forward to an evening with his wife.

"What are you doing for dinner tonight, Calvin?" Kaylin asked as she cut up some cucumber to make a salad. "Would you like to join us?"

Eating alone was a regular occurrence for me, so having a healthy meal with a wonderful family sounded like a great plan.

"I would love to," I replied, motioning to Nathan to pass me some plates to set the table.

"It's so interesting what you know about financial planning," Nathan said as he passed me some glasses. "I find it all so complex and confusing."

"We learned so much in school about history, geometry, spelling and math, but so little about the major life skill of managing money," Kaylin said, shaking her head.

Nathan reached over and put his arm around Kaylin. "Cal, we try hard to manage our money, but the financial stresses are putting some strain on our marriage."

Kaylin gently put her head on Nathan's shoulder. "Is it just us, Cal? Or are there others who find financial matters stressful?"

I looked deeply at both of them. "Financial stress is one of the leading causes of stress in people's lives, but people don't talk about it. You are not alone; there are countless arguments, stress leaves and bouts of depression caused by financial wellness issues. It is a big problem that we need to begin talking about," I said.

Justin came running into the kitchen with a yellow sponge ball in one hand and a black and brown Wilson baseball mitt on his other hand.

"No playing ball in the kitchen," Kaylin said as she moved towards Justin to lead him back into the living room.

Looking at this young man so excited about baseball made a me a little sad that I didn't yet have any grandchildren. I look upon Justin and Taylor like my own grandchildren. I want to see them grow up in a happy, healthy, and financially secure home.

"By the way, Cal, thank you so much for the advice on our mortgage insurance. We spoke to our agent last month and ended up getting some insurance," Nathan said as he helped put the salad together.

A couple months ago, on their last mortgage renewal, Nathan asked me about mortgage insurance. Should they get it, or not? I knew this was a big money-maker for the bank and offered peace of mind to borrowers, knowing that if they were to die, the mortgage would be paid off by the insurance proceeds. With this type of life insurance they had, the premium stayed the same, but the coverage dropped as the mortgage balance dropped, so every payment they made lowered how much of a benefit they would receive since the benefit always matched the mortgage balance. However, if they moved their mortgage to another financial institution for a better rate or better terms, they would likely have to reapply for the insurance.

One of the solutions that often comes up is term life insurance. This insurance is temporary insurance where the premium and coverage amount of the insurance stays the same for the term of the policy, which is normally ten to twenty years. Long enough for the bulk of the mortgage to be paid off. At the end of the term, the insured can normally renew it for another ten or twenty years at a higher rate. Eventually, the renewals stop at around age seventy-five or when the premiums just become too expensive for most people. This type of insurance pays out to the insured's beneficiaries instead of the bank, unlike bank mortgage insurance, which usually goes to directly pay off the mortgage. With personal term insurance, the beneficiary will be able to pay the mortgage off, or not, if they choose not to. They will likely have some cash left over once the mortgage is paid since the mortgage payments, reducing the mortgage balance, do not reduce the amount of insurance coverage since the insurance amount stays the same. Both the term insurance and bank mortgage insurance options are viable options and help to provide stability and allow the surviving spouse and kids to remain in the family home without having to sell it.

Insurance is another theoretical product. I can't remember how many people I have spoken to, usually men it seems, who say they don't need insurance on their mortgage because their wife will just sell the home and have lots of cash to pay rent and provide for their family. While to some it seems logical, what they fail to see is that having to sell the home quickly and in a time of emotional turmoil will cause the sale price to be less than it could be. Usually when people want to get maximum value for their home, they will spend some time doing repairs, repainting and searching for a new home. I can't imagine what this would be like as a single parent who just lost their spouse. This is just another example of seeing how the math adds up but missing the human element.

A few months ago when Kaylin, Nathan and I discussed this, they told me their mortgage payment was $1,400 per month. Strata fees, utilities, insurance, and property taxes amounted to another $550 per month. Nathan's paycheques were $4,000 per month while Kaylin brought in $3,500. I discussed with them that if all they had was insurance to cover the mortgage and no other life insurance, they would have a clear title house and no mortgage payment. However, since the mortgage payment was only $1,400 and Nathan and Kaylin brought in $4,000 and $3,500 respectively, they would still have $2,100 or $2,600 less per month than they do today. There were also the added stresses of going to work and taking care of the kids as a single parent if one of them passed away. They would still likely need to sell the house to make ends meet. I showed them on the back of a napkin.

Nathan's income: $4,000
Kaylin's income: $3,500
Mortgage payment: $1,400
Net income after the mortgage is
paid: $6,100

If Nathan dies:
Kaylin's income: $3,500
Mortgage payment: $0
Net income: $3,500—still $2,600 short,
even with a house with the mortgage paid off.

If Kaylin dies:
Nathan's income: $4,000
Mortgage payment: $0
Net income: $4,000—still $2,100 short,
even with a house with the mortgage paid off.

While mortgage insurance was a start, it was just the tip of the iceberg. I suggested they talk to their insurance agent about their needs outside of the mortgage.

They also each had a car loan. Nathan's grey Toyota Highlander cost him $410 per month and Kaylin's white Honda Civic had a payment of $389. They had insurance they bought at the dealership that would help pay the car loans off if one of them tragically died. If one of them passed away, the insurance on those loans would save them a car payment; however, that was still only about $400 each per month in cash flow. Even with their mortgage and both car loans insured, they would still be well short of their cash flow needs if one of them passed away.

Kaylin brought over the chicken and rice and Nathan brought the salad as we all sat down to begin our meal.

"How did the meeting go with your insurance agent?" I asked, tasting the rice.

"We talked a lot about the different types of insurance. We discussed mortgage insurance, temporary insurance, which he called term, and permanent insurance," Nathan said as he cut Justin's meat.

"That's good," I replied. "A number of people avoid the discussion about permanent insurance because of the cost and because of the length of the term, which is usually for the life of the insured person."

I poured some ranch dressing on my salad. "Permanent insurance is more expensive, but generally speaking, the premium and the amount of the insurance stays the same for the life of the policy, which is for the life of the insured. Generally, people end up focusing on term insurance. We call it term or temporary because it is usually for a set term of ten to twenty years and it is a temporary solution, as it usually expires prior to someone collecting on it if they live to a ripe old age," I said, enjoying the fresh salad.

"One of the reasons term insurance is so inexpensive is that it rarely pays out. Most of the time, people buy term insurance and never claim on it, because they outlive the policy or cancel it when they don't need it or when the premiums become unaffordable. Term insurance is less costly for the insurance company because of the lower percentage of payouts they have after the cancellations and expiries. Term insurance is a very good, low cost, temporary solution to protect people in situations like when their kids are young, still living at home," I said.

"The insurance agent also said it is good for protecting a person's income or paying off debt. He said term insurance can be used to help the surviving family to continue to receive income until retirement or to protect a temporary issue such as a loan or mortgage," Kaylin added as she placed Taylor in the high chair.

"Permanent insurance is a little different. It enables the same protection as term insurance but also can be used as a strategy to help people reduce taxes or allow them to give to charity when they are older," I said, remembering how we used it to help Henry and Jessica Walters leave money to the church.

"He said that permanent insurance can also do things like help to increase your estate or use as a strategy to increase your pension," Nathan added in.

"Actually, yes, you are right, I was able to help some folks from the Lakes use insurance to increase their pension," I said, thinking about how I helped Dale and Marie in unit two.

"We ended up getting permanent insurance for $50,000 and term insurance to replace each of our incomes, pay off the loans, and provide schooling for the kids in the event one of us passes away suddenly." Kaylin said.

"We were able to get all of this insurance for less than $200 per month. We added up the costs of the mortgage insurance and the insurance on the car loans and compared it with the benefits we would receive; it was clear that this was the right solution for us," Kaylin continued, glancing at Nathan.

"This gives me peace of mind, knowing that if something were to happen to Kaylin or me that the other person and the kids would be taken care of," Nathan said as he wiped Justin's mouth with a napkin.

"Another thing to consider," I started, "is with the insurance you purchased, you have the ability to convert some of the coverage every year from term to permanent. I would recommend that you convert 10% of your insurance every year from term to permanent. Converting 10% per year would allow you to have more permanent coverage as you get closer to retirement. This will keep costs down while you build your careers, and as you get closer to retirement, you can utilize the insurance to increase your estate, increase your pension or plan a large gift to a charity."

"Even though it is only $200 per month, it is still a lot of money. I am still not convinced that we can afford it," Nathan said, not looking up.

Kaylin's eyes widened and I could see she was not happy with Nathan's comment.

I took a bit more of a stern tone with Nathan. "Unfortunately, people will often not get insurance because of the cost and because it is optional. Car insurance and house insurance, if you have a mortgage, is mandatory; we just build that into the cost of the house or car. Life insurance, on the other hand, being optional, often ends up not being involved in people's financial plans. Have you ever heard the movie theatre story, Nathan?" I asked.

I told them the movie theatre story.

The Movie Theatre Story

A man walks into a movie theatre with his two young kids. As he walks down the aisle, he notices the lady that he buys his car insurance from sitting with her family. He waves to them as he continues down the aisle. Then, he spots the mortgage broker that gave them their mortgage. The man waves to him and his family and continues towards the front of the theatre. Two rows down they notice the young man that sold him his cell phone plan sitting with his young family. After waving to this young man and his family, the man and his kids go down and sit in the front row of the theatre.

In the middle of watching the movie, a fire breaks out in the theatre. People are screaming and running towards the exits. The man stands up and turns to his kids and says, "Stay right here. I am going to help the car insurance lady and her family out of the theatre. I will then go and help the mortgage broker and his family out and then I will make sure that the cell phone guy and his family are safe. But I promise you, once all of them are taken care of I will come back and protect you."

"Is that a realistic story?" I asked.

Nathan shook his head and scoffed. "That's ridiculous," he said, glancing at Kaylin.

"Really?" I asked. "Because without insurance, you're doing that, right now, financially. You're taking care of everyone else, but if there is an emergency, your family would not be protected. Your rationale is that you need to take care of everyone else first. You are putting your family behind everyone else."

"I think you need to realign your priorities, honey," Kaylin said as she finished her plate.

Nathan nodded, got up and began to clear the table.

After playing catch with Justin and talking baseball with Nathan and Kaylin, I called it a night and headed back home.

Nathan and Kaylin came by earlier than expected the next day with the kids. They handed me a diaper bag, the playpen and a collection of toys and books. It had been many years since I had to change diapers, and I was not looking forward to that part of this evening.

"We came a little early," Kaylin explained as she handed me a list of the foods the kids could eat. "We would like to ask you about saving for the kids' education. With all of our expenses, even though we make pretty good money, we just can't seem to find a way to save money for education savings."

I smiled and gave Kaylin a chuckle. "If there is one truth that I have learned, it is that it doesn't matter a person's income. If it's left unchecked, their lifestyle will grow to meet their income level, and in many cases exceed their income, causing them to build up unwanted debt. Many movie and sports stars making millions of dollars have gone bankrupt due to mismanaging their money and living beyond their means, even if it was millions of dollars per year."

I invited Kaylin and Nathan to come in and have a seat. "Let me ask you a question—what would happen if you came upon a large unplanned expense or an unexpected drop in income?"

"I don't know," Kaylin said. "I suspect we would have to reduce our expenses or use our credit cards or a line of credit to pay the bill or make ends meet."

I relaxed back into my chair. "Whenever we have a drop in income or come across an unexplained large expense, we have to adjust our lifestyle downward. In other words, we have to find a way to spend less money. If we don't, we end up taking on unwanted debt. Keeping our lifestyle in check and within our means is the surest way of staying out of debt."

Nathan sat up. "How do we go about adjusting our lifestyle downward?" he asked.

"The best way to do this is when you get paid, ensure that the first thing you pay is your own savings. Pay yourself first. Set some money aside into a savings account. With this money eliminated from spending, you will begin to adjust your lifestyle downward and live below your means. One of the easiest ways to do this is if you have a monthly payment reduced or eliminated, ensure you continue to make that payment, but pay it to yourself. If your car loan of $389 gets paid off, continue to make that payment to your savings. This will keep your lifestyle in check and will build up extra savings. If you get a pay increase, put part of that money automatically into savings," I explained.

"So I should start a savings program where I put money into a savings account every time I get paid. That is a good idea. As far as the loan goes, well, we have a while to go yet," Kaylin said as she adjusted in her seat.

"Another great way for this type of savings to may happen more often is to continue paying payroll taxes," I said.

"What does that mean?" asked Nathan as he glanced at Kaylin with a look of confusion.

"You see, on our paycheques, we have payroll taxes that include employment insurance, CPP contributions, union dues, and other deductions. Normally we don't even notice them, for most people they don't know how much they pay in payroll taxes, they only know how much they get paid into their bank account," I explained.

Kaylin nodded. "Yes, that is true. I am not sure how much comes off my cheque every payday, I only know what I get paid."

I pointed to my calendar. "Sometime during the year, if you make enough money, the employment insurance and CPP contributions end and your net pay goes up a little bit. This is because there is a maximum that everyone pays towards CPP and EI. Does that happen for you two?" I asked.

Nathan looked at Kaylin. "Yes, those end for both of us sometime in September. Our pay goes up by about $400 per month then," he said.

"That sounds about right," I replied. "For a lot of people, their paycheques go up and, you guessed it, they now have 'found' money and end up increasing their lifestyle, spending that money on a new whatchamacallit or thingamajig and end up just blowing it."

"Hey, that's us." Nathan snorted and we all laughed.

"My suggestion is to continue to pay those payroll taxes, which work out to about $400 per month, for the final four months of the year. Instead of paying the payroll taxes to the government, put the $400 monthly into an RESP for the kids, for a total of $1,600. With the government grants that come along with the RESP, you should be able to put in close to $2,000 into the education fund. If you can resist the temptation to use your 'found' money, you can start to build a nice education fund for the kids without reducing your lifestyle."

A smile drew across Kaylin's face. "I will make sure that we watch our paystubs and when we know when the payroll taxes get reduced, I can then set up a regular bi-weekly contribution to an RESP, on our paydays, to spend our 'found' money."

Nathan rubbed his chin. "I think what you're saying is that by being proactive, every time we come into some extra money like payroll taxes, loan payments and pay raises, we should be proactively moving that money out of our spending account and into savings or RESPs," he said proudly.

"Exactly right." I smiled.

"Oh my gosh, look at the time!" Kaylin exclaimed, jumping up. "We need to head out for dinner."

Nathan and Kaylin gave the kids a hug, thanked me again and headed out for dinner.

I put the playpen onto the area rug in the living room and placed Taylor in there. She was content staring at the plastic farm animals hanging off the mobile above her head while she sucked on the pacifier as if it were her favourite thing in the world. Justin brought his colouring book and we proceeded to make a blue castle, a purple princess and green sky. The orange horse we made next turned out to be Justin's favourite. As I played with these beautiful young kids, it helped me reflect on the love that I have for my own kids. I remembered when they were little, colouring purple princesses and playing with their favourite toys. I could also clearly see the love that Kaylin and Nathan had for these wonderful kids.

I sat there, pondering the thoughts of them out at the winery for dinner, how they were working so hard saving for and protecting their kids. This was a long road for them, saving monthly, paying bills to get ahead. Financial freedom, it seemed, was different for everyone. For Nathan and Kaylin Williamson, their whole world and financial freedom had little to do with how much money they had in the bank or how big their house was. Instead, it was to protect and provide for these little gems. If they could love each other and love these young kids, they would be able to provide for their family for a long time. Staying together would help them reach their financial goals. Money was an enabler for them. Something as simple as continuing payroll taxes would help them reach their version of financial freedom.

Spending money on things like insurance stinks, but when it is on your own kids, it's like changing diapers; it just doesn't smell as bad. It seems that financial freedom for them wasn't how much money they had, it was love. Love for each other and love for their children.

Key Learnings

- Review all of your life insurance regularly and consider the long-term benefits of permanent insurance
- Remember the movie theatre story—are you funding the important things first?
- Take advantage of pay increases and temporary increases like maxed CPP contributions to fund an emergency fund or contribute to important savings like RESPs
- Take time to align your financial values with your spouse—and keep your relationship strong

CHAPTER 4

Move Your Wallet to the Other Pocket

Jason Vickers slammed the gate shut and stomped his way up towards unit five. The fit thirty-five-year-old knew that the golf season was coming to an end, and so was his means of making good money selling golf clubs. Jason was a good athlete, excelling in golf, tennis, and just about any sport he has ever tried. Unfortunately, the one sport he was not good at was money management.

Jason came in to see me at my office three months ago, telling me about his financial problems. This man had a lot going for him; however, like many Canadians, financial stress was taking a toll on his mental health. At 6'2" and 190 lbs, Jason was a striking, intimidating figure. You noticed Jason when he walked into a room; his striking eyes made you take notice. As a single man, Jason's social life was very busy and he knew all of the local bars and hiking spots. This served him well with women. The parade of young beautiful women that entered and left the Lakes, coming and going from unit five, was like a Victoria's Secret modelling runway. On the surface, it seemed he had it all together.

In the summertime, Jason worked selling golf clubs for the Golf Shoppe in the high-end district of Kelowna called the Mission. His smooth confident smile served him well, and he did very well as a commission-based salesperson. In the winter, and some evenings during the rest of the year, he worked at the local gym as a personal trainer. This, I believe, was where he met his female friends. If you were to meet Jason, you would notice his masculine confidence and assuredness. Unfortunately, his lack of financial acuity had caused him stress, and I could see his confidence waning.

Jason came to see me that day in late spring to discuss his problems. He drove a beautiful black Ford F-150 that he had bought two years ago. With a great season of bonuses selling high-end golf clubs like Pings, TaylorMades and Callaways, he managed to save up $20,000 as a down payment. Unfortunately, he still owed $45,000 on the truck. He had five years left on his $850/month loan, and it was causing him some stress. Cash flow was also a problem, as he had his $9,200 student loan, which he was paying $200 per month on. His credit card, which had maxed out its $10,000 limit, charged him an interest rate of 19.9%. Unfortunately, with two jobs, rarely was enough tax withheld, and at the end of the year there was a tax problem. Jason owed the CRA $4,000 and would owe more in April when he filed his taxes again.

With my career in financial services, I knew where this was headed. CRA would send a notice to the bank to garnish his bank account to begin paying the taxes he was owed. Eventually, every time he made a deposit, his money would be frozen and sent to the CRA. Eventually he would not be able to have a regular bank account and would end up going to a payday cash store to cash his cheque, where they would charge him 3% to cash his cheque.

A lifetime of misguided priorities had caused Jason to go into debt. $150 dinner dates, Mexican vacations, and a love for expensive golf courses weighed on Jason's financial situation. At this point, Jason had been renting unit five now for just about three years. He definitely added some fun and colourfulness to the Lakes and kept everyone laughing whenever we had our complex barbeque.

I watched Jason continue to stomp his way up to his unit.

"Jason!" I called out as he kicked a rock into the garden. "How are you doing?"

Jason just looked at me. I could see the sadness and disappointment in his eyes.

"Hi Cal, sorry if I was loud coming in the gate," he said with his jaw clenched and brow furrowed.

"What's going on?" I asked.

A light spattering of rain had fallen on Jason's t-shirt and the rain on his face accentuated his sad eyes.

"I just saw Tanya holding hands with another guy, walking towards his BMW. She was laughing and kissing him. She was with me just this weekend. We had a great time. I took her to Brown's for dinner and we had a great night," he replied dejectedly.

I understood his hurt, but that very situation had been reversed many times. He had done the exact same thing to several women in the past. I hid my sense of irony and invited him inside my unit for a scotch. Jason and I shared a taste for good scotch. I preferred Glenfiddich, while his favourite was Bowmore.

"So, Tanya's the one?" I asked, already knowing the answer.

"No, she clearly isn't. What the hell, Cal? I work hard and play hard, I'm having a great time, but I am so unhappy. I live in a beautiful part of the world, meet lots of people, and play golf regularly, but I am discontent with life."

"What are your goals, Jason? What kind of life would make you happy?" I asked as I brought out two tumblers and poured some twelve-year-old Glenfiddich over ice.

"Cal, I would like to meet a nice woman, someone who loves me for more than a month, a life where I can settle down, buy a house and get on with my life. I just can't seem to get ahead. Now I have the CRA calling me constantly. My cards are still maxed. Work is going well, I love both of my jobs, but they never take enough tax off. What is wrong with them?" Jason took his first swallow of scotch.

After being in financial planning for several years, there were a few truths that I had come to learn. Almost everyone that I met with financial difficulties seemed to have a student loan and they tend to think tax problems were someone else's fault. I haven't figured out the link between people that have financial problems and student loans, but I believed there was a correlation somewhere there. Not everyone that had a student loan had financial problems, but it seemed that most people I met with financial problems had a student loan. As far as the tax problems went, this was common amongst people with multiple jobs.

"Okay, Jason, do you want some help?" I asked, lifting the tumbler to my lips so I could taste the oakiness of the scotch.

"Of course I do, Cal, I am at my wits' end," he replied. Jason was almost in tears. The stress was truly affecting him. "Okay." He sighed. "Let's talk about the tax problem first."

"When we file our taxes, we get non-refundable tax credits. This basically means that our first, roughly, $11,000 of income in BC works out tax free. That basic personal tax credit generally goes up every year. Everything else is taxable. The next $30,000 or so is taxed at about 20%, and then it goes up from there. With your total income being $61,000, the last $20,000 you earned was taxed at roughly 30%. What this means for you, Jason, is that on your income of $61,000, you will pay nothing on your first $11,000, $6,000 of tax on your next $30,000, then the last $20,000, at 30%, you will pay another, roughly, $6,000 in tax. Overall, you will pay $12,000 on $61,000 worth of income, making your average tax rate about 20%. Let me show you on a napkin."

I pulled out another napkin, which seemed to be my favourite medium of financial planning and jotted down what I meant.

Income: $61,000
First $11,000 = Tax Free
Next $30,000 – 20% = $6,000
Next $20,000 – 30% = $6,000

Total Income = $61,000.
Tax payable = $12,000 for a total of 20% on average.

"Okay, Cal," Jason said. "That makes sense, but why do I owe money all the time?"

"The problem you're running into is that the Golf Shoppe only pays you $41,000 and the gym pays you $20,000. The Golf Shoppe assumes you get the basic personal tax credit making your first roughly $11,000 free and withholds 20% on your next $30,000 for a total of $6,000, which is correct."

I wrote it down for him on the napkin.

Golf Shoppe

Income: $41,000
Tax free: $11,000
Taxable income: $30,000
Tax withheld at 20% = $6,000

"That makes sense." Jason refilled his tumbler.

"The problem arises," I continued, "when the gym thinks the same thing. They pay you $20,000, assuming your first $11,000 is tax-free because of the basic personal tax credit, and they withhold 20% on your next $9,000 for a total of $1,800."

Again, I wrote on the napkin.

Gym

Income: $20,000
Tax free (so the gym assumes): $11,000
Taxable Income: $9,000
Tax withheld at 20% = $1,800
Total tax withheld between the gym
and Golf Shoppe is $7,800

"You end up filing your income tax at the end of the year where you should have paid $12,000, but only $6,000 has been withheld from the Golf Shoppe and just a mere $1,800 was withheld at the gym for a total of $7,800. You end up with a tax bill for $4,200. Unless you do something about it, you will continue to owe the CRA every year. There are two problems here. The first is that both employers are assuming that you receive the basic personal tax credit, when it can only be applied once. The second is that you are paying tax at the lower rate when $20,000 should be taxed at 30% and not 20%," I explained.

"Basically, what you're telling me is that one job's payroll does not know about the other job, and since I haven't told them, they are doubling up on the basic personal tax credit and they are calculating the tax wrong?" Jason said. His expression was a combination of success and despair at the same time.

"This is very common amongst people who have multiple jobs," I explained. "It happens more that you think."

"Is there anything I can do about it?" he asked.

"You have two choices. The first choice is you can set aside $333 per month and then remit that to the government. You actually owe this money, so setting it aside will allow you to have it to pay at the end of the year. Some people will say that this is the best choice, because you will earn interest on this money and therefore you will make a little bit of interest. The second choice is you talk to your employers, fill out a TD1 form and have them withhold the extra tax. My suggestion to you is the latter. It takes good financial self-discipline to do the first, and, theoretically, it is a good choice. Unfortunately, we are human beings and have difficulty with the self-discipline part of money. Most crimes and political motivations are to do with money, so I think our society has proven that financial self-discipline is not our strong suit."

"No kidding," murmured Jason as he rolled his eyes.

I smiled. "I would suggest going to the payroll departments of your employers and asking for the TD1 form to withhold taxes. Unfortunately, regardless of which you choose, your take-home pay is going to get reduced by $333 per month on average."

Regrettably, I thought to myself, Jason does not have a lot of self-discipline and may have trouble saving the $333 per month on his own. Some of his friends or some advisors may counsel him on saving instead of giving the money to the government so that he earns the interest on the money. While the math works on this, in an effort to save the roughly $25 in interest he would get in a year, it could cause him, being as financially undisciplined as he is, to owe the government much more than the $25 he would have earned in interest.

Jason sighed audibly. "My financial problems are getting worse, Cal."

"Things will get worse before they get better," I replied empathetically.

He grunted out a laugh. "That's encouraging."

I thumped him encouragingly on the knee. "Now, let's talk about increasing your cash flow. We know that you earn $61,000 per year but after all of your payroll taxes, including CPP, EI, staff fund contributions and benefits deductions, you bring home $3,500 per month for a total of $42,000 per year. The first step in getting out of debt is to stop getting into debt," I tell him.

Jason, who had started appreciating the nice scotch a little more, said, "What's next?"

"The next thing you need to do is start building an emergency fund, putting $200 per paycheque into this fund. This way when an emergency comes up, and it will, you will go into this fund rather than deeper into debt.

Emergencies come up all the time, even the expected ones. Things like car repairs, needing a new TV or buying gifts," I explain.

"Are you kidding me! How am I supposed to do that?" Jason put his head in his hands. "I already have too many bills to pay, you have my income reduced by $333 per month in taxes, and now you have me putting aside $200 per paycheque. That works out to $400 per month, plus the money for taxes, and you have me trying to find $733 in extra money every month!" Jason's massive frame started to tense up.

"The $333 per month will come directly off your paycheque, and the $200 per paycheque for your emergency fund needs to automatically transfer to a savings account on the day you get paid. It's the first thing that comes out of your account. You need to put it aside. This is called paying yourself first." I mustered up as much confidence as I could to keep talking him through this. "Jason," I said, "see my wallet?" I reached back and pulled out my wallet. "I always keep it in the back left pocket of my jeans."

I then moved my wallet over to the back right pocket of my jeans. I then reach back into my empty left pocket of my jeans I exclaim "Oh my goodness! My money, it's gone! Oh no, I have no money!" I said with a wry smile.

Jason laughed.

"You see, Jason, my money is not gone, it's just in a different place, the same as your money will be. For the first two to three times you do this, you will likely dip into this money. That is okay, it will take time to get used to this lifestyle adjustment. You will soon find that your lifestyle will adjust and you will leave $50 in there. Then the next two weeks it will be $75, and continue until eventually the entire $200 will stay in there. It will take some time for you to adjust, but eventually you will find an emergency fund with hundreds or thousands of dollars in it. When you find yourself in a financial emergency, as we all do at some point during the year, you will have enough to pay for it in your emergency fund. You will need to give yourself time to adjust to this new lifestyle," I said.

"Now, let's talk about that truck of yours." I raised an eyebrow at him. "It is a very nice truck, but some people may say that with a big truck like that you are, ahem, compensating for something else," I said with a laugh.

Jason was not amused. "I love that truck. I don't want to get rid of it."

"Jason, at $850 per month, that truck is a big part of your problem. You chose to put $20,000 down on that truck and pay $850 per month. You could have instead bought a $15,000 vehicle with payments of just $350 per month for four years instead of the seven years you are paying on the truck. Had you done that and put the $500 difference per month away for the past two years, you would have saved $12,000 plus the $20,000 you had already saved. With interest, that would have grown to almost $35,000. That's enough to put down on an apartment or townhouse. If you continue down this path, in five years you will be deeper in debt and have a truck worth $20,000. If you stop now and sell the truck, you can get $45,000 for it, pay off that loan, and cut your losses. You can then get a four-year loan at $350 per month for a used car, and you will have freed up $500 per month to put towards your other debts. You have a choice to make: have a really nice truck for the next few years or start digging your way out of debt and saving for a house."

Jason stared out the window, watching the rain fall. His look told me that he was sad to lose his truck, but combating his financial stress was important to him.

I went on. "Building up your emergency fund will help you to stop going deeper into debt. Any abnormal expenses should come out of there, also, your extra savings on your truck loan, as well as reduced dinners and golf, will need to go to pay down credit cards and loans. Another thing, Jason." I leaned forward. "Talk to the CRA. Get a plan in place and work with them. Most creditors, including the CRA, are reasonable. It is when there is no payment and no communication that they become unreasonable. By getting in control of your finances, and proactively making the call to CRA, your stress will start to diminish."

Jason's eyes softened and I saw the tough love starting to have an effect on him.

"Jason. You are a great guy. Your value does not come in the form of the car you drive or the $150 dinners. If you teach people that your value comes in these material things, that is how they will treat you. We teach people how to treat us. Refocusing your efforts on long-term financial success is going to help you. Paying yourself first and focusing on staying out of debt will set you on a path to good financial habits."

Over the years, counselling people to pay themselves first and building up an emergency fund has, one hundred percent of the time, started with an incredulous, mouth-wide, gaping stare with a look that said, "I came here for help and it turns out you are an idiot." But most of the people who have done this have successfully lowered their lifestyle and, like a snowball, worked their way out of debt. Once they rid themselves of their debts and are in control of their situation, they are happier and have less stress. Without these measures, the snowball works the other way and the debt builds up.

"This is going to be tough, Cal." Jason took another drink of the $90 bottle of scotch I provided.

"Jason, you will have to reduce your dinners to $75, play on some cheaper golf courses, and drink Canadian whisky, while driving a Honda Civic instead of a Ford F-150. In five years, you will be forty. You have two choices. You can be in debt, owing the government lots of money and driving a fully paid for seven-year-old Ford F-150, dating women who value you for the fancy dinners and the truck, or you can be debt free, buying your first home, and living a lifestyle with less financial stress. And trust me, if you do this, when you are fifty you will experience financial freedom."

Jason finished his scotch, put down the glass, leaned over, and gave me a hug. I could tell he truly appreciated the honesty I shared with him.

Jason had a lot of work ahead of him. For him, financial freedom was about finding a woman he loved and who loved him for who he was. He wanted to be able to have some stability in his life. He didn't need to have a million dollars, he just needed to find his value on the inside, instead of the outside.

Key Learnings

- Move your wallet to the other pocket—putting money into a different account doesn't mean it's gone—it's just in another place
- Are you buying things you don't want, to impress people you don't really care about?
- Build an emergency fund while paying down debt to stop going into debt
- If you have multiple jobs, review the taxes being taken off to ensure you are prepared when you file your taxes at the end of the year

CHAPTER 5

The $800 Jacket

I turned the corner from Keith Street and begin walking down Brian Avenue towards the lake. Okanagan Lake was the big, majestic jewel of the valley. There were beautiful wooden walkways and sandy beaches up and down the lake. For those of us who grew up in the lower mainland, we fully appreciated the plethora of parking available around the lakes, as opposed to the lakes in the lower mainland, where, if you didn't get there early enough, you had to park a kilometre away to get to the beach.

The stories of Ogopogo sightings and all of the dinner cruise ships full of drunk college students made for interesting stories with tall tales and some tales that you wished were tall. Some things you just can't unsee. The college in Kelowna attracted people from all over Canada; not only was it a good learning institution, it was in a beautiful part of the country well known for its wineries, golf courses, and parties.

Emily Selvage was a pretty twenty-year-old with long brunette hair, a sharp wit, and lots of experience in the party life that Kelowna offers. She completed her two-year program at the college and then started work as an insurance agent at McMurchy Insurance Services on Keith. After so many years of living with her parents, Emily was getting that itch that a lot of young people get. She wanted to get out of her parents' house and get her own place. When I pushed her as to why she wanted to get out of a place where she was paying only $350 per month to her parents, she said she wanted her freedom. She wanted a place where she could paint the walls whatever colour she wished and stop flushing rent down the toilet. Emily has a good head on her shoulders, and a pretty good mouth on her as well. She was never afraid to speak her mind.

As I walked under a sunny cloudless sky down Keith to buy car insurance from Emily, I couldn't help but think that car insurance was one of those things that everyone needs but doesn't really think about. The outrageous cost of $1,800 per year for my $25,000 asset, versus the $600 I paid for insurance on my house, made my head hurt, but it was necessary. There are certain assets that we need to insure, but we fail to do so. I remembered speaking with our branch management team and telling them the money machine story.

The Money Machine

Close your eyes. Imagine a place in your home that you rarely go. It could be the closet in the bedroom downstairs, it could be that little cupboard in the laundry room, or maybe it is next to the freezer in the garage. Do you have that place in your head? Now imagine down in the corner is a machine about the size of a toaster oven. This machine prints out money, legal tender that you can spend. Can you see it? Can you hear the machine? This machine runs twenty-four hours a day, seven days a week, printing money. Every fourteen days you go down and collect the money. This machine prints out the equivalent to your salary, in cash, every fourteen days. This machine is totally legal and quietly prints out money. Can you see the machine, can you hear the machine?

Now open your eyes.

Here is my question: How much would you insure it for? A hundred thousand dollars, five hundred thousand, a million?

Well, this machine is you, or your significant other. You go to work every day and earn money every day. If you or your significant other died or got injured, the machine would be broken. How much do you have your money machine insured for?

This story was meant to put things into perspective. We insure our homes, which are an asset worth likely somewhere between three hundred and eight hundred thousand dollars, but our ability to earn income is our biggest asset. So, a forty-five-year-old bank manager making one hundred thousand dollars per year would earn well in excess of two million dollars between now and age sixty-five, yet she would balk at disability or critical illness insurance. The asset that critical illness and disability insurance covered was often overlooked, but this "asset"—our ability to earn income—can be worth millions. Here I was, walking to McMurchy Insurance to lay down $1,800 for my $25,000 asset and the liability that went with it. As I pulled on the handle, I heard that familiar voice.

"Hey Mr. Bennett! You lost?"

"Hi Emily," I replied, "I need to get car insurance."

"You are insuring that very average car? Aren't you some big executive at the bank? How come you drive a Toyota Rav4?" she quipped.

It was interesting, because most bank executives I met drove BMWs, Porsches or Mercedes, but most financial planners I met drove modest cars. To invest that much money into a depreciating asset was very difficult for me to get my head around. Make no mistake, I liked nice cars and love fast cars, but unless I had money to burn, I preferred investing in appreciating assets and not depreciating assets.

"What kind of car do you want, Emily?" I asked with a smile.

"I would like to get a new car, a convertible," she replied.

"I see. How much do you think that car will cost you?"

"Well, I think that I could get it for about forty-five thousand, a nice one! That works out to about $590 per month. I was talking with the dealership and they have new eight-year loans that will allow me to get a really nice car," she replied. "Better than what you are driving," she said with that mischievous smile.

"So, you will have a car that will cost you $590 per month for eight years. So how much will that car cost you altogether?" I asked.

Emily pulled out her calculator. "Well let's see, $590 per month will be $7,080 per year, so all in all it will cost me $7,080 per year for eight years. Therefore, it will cost me a total $56,640," she said, proud of her math.

"You are pretty good with a calculator," I replied. "But you are actually wrong if you include opportunity cost in your calculation. You see, you could buy a $20,000 car today and it would cost you about $243 per month instead. Instead, what if you bought the $20,000 car? If you took the difference between the $590 you will pay for your fancy car and the $243 for the average car, you will be saving about $347 per month. If you took that $347 per month and put it into an investment that earned 5% over those eight years, you would have just over $41,000. Therefore, in eight years, you will be twenty-eight years old with $41,000 in the bank. If you left that money in invested until you were sixty-five at the same rate of 5%, that $41,000 will grow to over $249,000."

Emily looked impressed.

"You see, Emily, the time value of money is so important to think about. This car is not costing you just $590 per month, it will cost you almost a quarter of a million dollars over the long term. So, the difference between your fancy car and your average car is actually $249,000."

"So, what you are saying," Emily said excitedly, "is that I should be careful with how much I invest in something that will depreciate in value and focus on something that will increase in value. And at my young age I will be able to use the magic of compound interest to make it grow."

"That's right, Emily! If you balance your wants and needs of today with future dollars in making purchasing decisions, you can really get ahead financially. We still need things like cars, appliances and furniture, but spending a few minutes thinking about opportunity cost will help you with your financial goals in the future."

"Now, Emily, I have to insure my 'very average car,' which, by the way, carries my kayaks and gets me from point A to point B very well. It's also great on the snowy highways, thank you very much. By the way, how are your parents doing?"

Kelly and Brett Selvage had owned unit seven at the Lakes for several years. They were very nice people, and they had their hands full with Emily. Kelly and Brett had sent Emily to talk to me about saving money a few times. Emily was very smart, quick-witted and driven. If she focused those brains and that wit on her goals, she would be very successful in life.

"They are as big pains as ever, still cashing my rent cheque every month, while I toil away selling insurance."

I couldn't help but laugh at Emily's wit as I sat down at her desk.

Emily's situation reminded me of my own daughter. She was living with me and working as a server in a local sushi restaurant. I didn't need the rent money, but I knew she needed to get used to paying rent. I charged her 32% of her income, up to $800 per month. The 32% number comes from the Gross Debt Service Ratio calculation that banks use when calculating how much a person can borrow when they purchase a house. My daughter complained to her friends about how much rent I charged her. Little did she know that I was actually saving that money in a savings account for her. I could have just charged her $300, but she could afford the larger amount and she needed to adjust her lifestyle to prepare her for living on her own. At the end of the year that she lived with me, I gave my daughter the $8,500 that she had paid in rent. I explained this to my friend Ryan, but Ryan said he wished he was in the financial situation that I was and that he needed the $300 rent that his daughter paid. We sat down and discussed his daughter's finances and it turns out she earned about $1,800 per month. Ryan bumped up the rent for his daughter to 32% of her income, $576, kept the $300 and put the $276 difference into a savings account for her. After a year, Ryan saved over $3,000 for his daughter and he was pleased that it helped to give her a head start. I loved what Ryan said to me afterwards: "Charging kids low rent doesn't help anyone. Charging closer to a regular rent payment and putting the excess that I don't need into savings not only prepares her for the future in managing money, but also provides her with a good start in life."

I looked at Emily with the face that my own daughter doesn't like. I raised my eyebrows, pursed my lips and said "You are getting a pretty good deal, paying $350 per month. I don't think you could find a place in Kelowna for less than a thousand." Emily knew I was right, but she still had a frustrated look on her face.

"I know that I could buy my own place if I only had a down payment, and then I could stop flushing rent money down the toilet. My friend Dana just bought a place, and she only pays $1,200 per month for her mortgage. I make pretty good money here, and I know I can be manager someday, so I can afford it," she said sternly.

"Do you have savings now?" I asked.

"I don't have any savings in my bank account, but I have an RRSP here at work with $4,000 in it. I can't touch it though until I retire."

"So how do you think you can possibly afford to pay a mortgage, strata fees, property taxes, utilities, and other expenses when you can't even save any money?" I said as I nodded at the beautiful $800 Canada Goose jacket sitting on the back of her chair.

"Oh, if it's for a mortgage, I would find a way. I just need to get out of that house. My mom is always nagging me to clean up, and my dad makes dumb jokes all the time. I can find a way."

"Well," I said, "I think you can as well."

Emily raised her eyebrows and gave me a little smile. A look of gratification.

"You can buy a three-bedroom starter condo on the outskirts of town for about $350,000. With 5% down, your mortgage payment will be about $1,300 per month, strata about $250 per month, and utilities and insurance another $200 per month. Your housing costs would be about $1,750 per month. So, all you need to do is put down $17,500 as a down payment, move that $350 per month you are now paying to $1,750 and boom, Bob's your uncle."

"Ha ha, Mr. Bennett, where am I going to come up with that money, and how am I going to afford a payment like that?" Emily asked in a sarcastic tone.

"You say that you think you can afford a mortgage payment of $1,200 per month, if you stop buying $800 jackets and blowing your money on movies and eating out. I agree with you. So, I would suggest you start doing that now. Begin paying $850 per month 'rent' into an RRSP. This, along with the rent you are currently paying will be the same as if you were paying $1,200 for a mortgage. This is the difference between what you think you can afford and what your rent is."

Emily nodded slowly.

"I agree, Emily, you can pay that kind of payment, you just need to make it happen. Over the course of a year you will save $10,200, and in eighteen months you will have $15,300. If you put this money into an RRSP, you will also get 20% back, or around $3,000 on your taxes. By also putting that money into savings, in eighteen months you will have saved about $18,000, enough to put down on your condo. Using the homebuyer's plan, you can pull that money out of your RRSP as a down payment."

"Really, I can do that, Mr. Bennett?"

"Yes, you can, Emily. Now the matter of the $1,750 for the mortgage and other costs. I doubt that a girl like you has any friends," I said with a wry smile.

Emily stuck her tongue out at me.

"But if you did, you could rent out the other two rooms to them for seven hundred each. This would be fourteen hundred and you are back to paying your $350 per month as you are now."

"That sounds pretty easy, Mr. Bennett. I have lots of friends that would love to share an apartment and $700 is pretty affordable rent. But I still have the problem of living with someone else and putting away that much is tough," Emily said as she pondered the advice.

"This is where priorities come in, Emily. What does financial freedom mean to you? Does it mean having nice jackets, fifty-dollar dinners and drinks every weekend, or does it mean having your own place, out from under your parents' roof, investing in an appreciating asset? And the difference between living with your parents and living with your friends are two things. First, your friends will be much more fun, with likely fewer dad jokes, and second: you will be the landlord."

Emily grinned at the thought.

"There is one thing, though. You mention flushing $350 per month down the toilet in rent. Well, interest on a mortgage, property taxes and strata fees may be a different toilet but will end up in the same sewer. The benefit of home ownership is that long term, historically, real estate prices rise. If your property rises or falls you get the benefit or cost of 'leverage.' If your $350,000 property rises by 10%, then it is worth $385,000. With a mortgage of $332,500, which is the $350,000 purchase price less the $17,500 you put down, you have 'equity' of $52,500, which means that you tripled your money. That is pretty good."

"Sounds good to me!" said Emily.

I nodded. "This is what makes real estate such a great investment. On the other hand, if your property value falls by 10% and becomes worth $315,000, and you owe $332,500, you would be in a 'negative equity' position. Over time, your mortgage will get paid down and real estate will likely rise, so you want to make sure you are in it for the long term. Remember, this whole plan starts with you having a mindset of paying market rent, while still having the benefit of living at home. Open an RRSP at your bank or credit union and have them automatically transfer $425 every two weeks when you get paid. If you truly want this, you have to make some sacrifices and change your priorities. It is achievable. The first step is to get that money out of your bank account. If it is not there, you won't spend it."

I could see Emily's mind racing a mile a minute as she logged into her online banking and started to look up RRSPs. "Wow, thanks for the advice, Mr. Bennett. It seems that being a nerd has its upside after all," she said with a wry smile.

"By the way," I said, "tell me about your RRSP."

"It is invested in five-year high interest savings. My boss said I should invest it that way because he lost so much money in mutual funds during the financial crisis. He says the safest place to put the money is in savings. I earn three percent, which he said is a pretty good rate," she said proudly.

I always shook my head when I saw people give out bad advice based on their bad decisions. Many people panicked during the financial crisis. The market dropped thirty percent and they sold, and then the market fell another twenty percent and they walked around like peacocks, thinking they made such an astute financial decision. But they never bought back in when it fell. I have rarely seen people buy back in when the market drops further. It's easy to see why, when the market falls further it's because people feel more pessimistic about stocks, so they wait until things *feel* better. But that only happens after the market recovers. At three percent, it would take them a very long time to make up the thirty percent they lost. Had they stayed in, they would have made all of their money back and more in a relatively short period of time. The market, and investors, reacted similarly to other crisis like '74, '87, 2008 and others. Now the boss was doling out advice to this young lady in an effort to help her to not make the same mistakes that he made. The problem was not that the mistake he made was investing in market-based investments; the mistake was selling out when the market went down.

"Emily, I want to explain to you the power of compound interest. Have you heard of the rule of seventy-two?"

"No," she replied.

"The rule of seventy-two is this: if you take your interest rate and divide it into seventy-two, that is how long it takes for your investment to double. You are currently earning 3%, and seventy-two divided by three is twenty-four, so it will take twenty-four years for your investment to double. Using the rule of seventy-two and starting at age twenty, your $4,000 investment will double in twenty-four years, at your age forty-four, to $8,000. It will then double again to $16,000 in another twenty-four years when you turn age sixty-eight. Not bad for doing nothing."

"Not bad," echoed Emily.

"Let's do the same calculation at 6%. With a good diversified mutual fund, historically, 6% is a pretty safe long-term growth rate. In this case, seventy-two divided by six is twelve. Your investment will double in twelve years. Your $4,000 will double to $8,000 at age thirty-two, double again to $16,000 at age forty-four, again to $32,000 at age fifty-six and double again to $64,000 at age sixty-eight. This was four times what you would make in a savings account. The rule of seventy-two, Emily, is one of the easiest and best investment concepts, especially for young people. Put your money into a mutual fund and let it grow. It will go up and down and probably never make exactly six percent in any one year, but the ups and downs will average out as long as you stay invested. Tell your friends about the rule of seventy-two and you will be able to help them make lots of money over time for their retirement savings."

I took one of the sticky notes she used and drew it out for her.

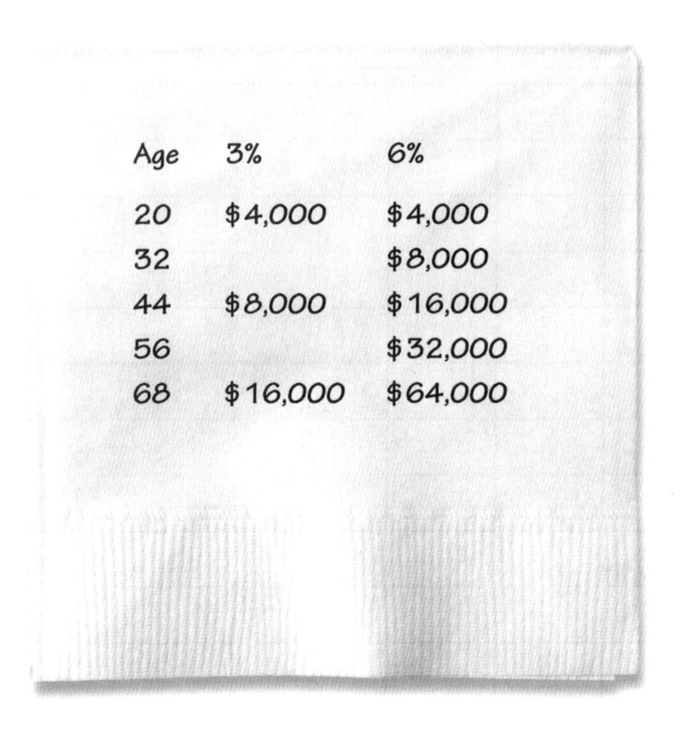

Age	3%	6%
20	$4,000	$4,000
32		$8,000
44	$8,000	$16,000
56		$32,000
68	$16,000	$64,000

"Thanks, Mr. Bennett." Emily took the sticky note. "I will go online and look for some managed money solutions. Do you have any recommendations?"

"Actually, if you get a chance, talk to Daryl Jagger in unit one, he is a financial advisor and he can walk through the different investments available and give you some advice."

With my car insurance in hand, I walked back up Keith Avenue towards Brian Street thinking about the smart and driven young lady that Emily was. To master a couple of simple concepts at such a young age would make such a difference in her financial life. Just taking the time to treat her like the young adult she was and give her some advice could make all the difference.

Walking with the sun in my face, I reminisced about all of the times I had shown the rule of seventy-two to young people, parents, bank staff and friends, I wondered how many had taken the advice. This simple concept could help start someone in the right direction. Financial freedom for Emily was about being in control of her own destiny: getting her own place, feeling good about herself. I guess financial freedom for her was about loving her independent self.

Key Learnings:

- Remember the Rule of 72: 72 divided by the interest rate you are earning equals how many years it will take for your investment to double.
- Help your kids by preparing them to manage their money. Charging higher rents and helping them to manage their lifestyle, while saving the excess rent, will help them get a leg up financially.
- The time value of money means that the difference between a $ 20,000 car and a $ 40,000 is worth much more than $ 20,000 in the future.

CHAPTER 6

The Greatest Job in The World

Daryl Jagger and I were driving my Toyota Rav4 north down highway ninety-seven, chatting about the Blue Jays' lack of pitching, but great young infield they have. Guerrero, Biggio, and Bichette were a good future for the Jays. Vladimir Guerrero Jr hit a record ninety-one home runs in the 2019 home run derby. I'd been to the batting cage myself, and I couldn't swing the bat ninety-one times without my arms falling off, let alone hit ninety-one home runs. The potential that this young man has is very exciting.

It was rare to find as big of a baseball fan as me, but Daryl Jagger was also a huge fan. Two years ago, I checked off my bucket list and became the on-field PA announcer for our local minor league ball team. Although this was just a volunteer gig, announcing was a dream come true. I spent my youth on the ball field as a bat boy, excited about watching the Commercial Bears play the Arms in my hometown. When I was not announcing, Daryl and I had taken to going to games, which was where I got to know him.

At age thirty-two, he was a financial planner for the bank. Daryl's job was to meet with bank customers, find out what their goals were, and suggest a plan to help them reach their goals. I had been in wealth management for twenty-five years and still found this to be the best business in the world. Unfortunately, Daryl struggled with it. He was not confident in his advice, didn't know how to obtain new customers very well, and was trying to build a good business while keeping his bosses happy. Darryl and I had been meeting for six months and were now having dinner on a monthly basis to talk about the wealth management business and how he can succeed in it. Our favourite dinner spot was The Keg. We would go and order the same appetizers and drinks every time. I ordered the escargot along with a nice merlot and Daryl ordered the baked shrimp mushroom caps with a dark Rum and Coke. The house merlot was not the most expensive wine, but it was one of my favourites.

I raised the long-stemmed wine glass to my lips, had a taste, and asked, "So, how did things work out for you after the pandemic recovery?"

"I appreciate your help, Cal. Things worked out great. I ended up with more referrals, but more importantly, my clients ended up making it through very well."

Back in mid-March 2020, the market had tanked quickly as the pandemic was taking hold in Italy and was moving quickly to the United States. Markets were falling ten to twelve percent per day and I had inquired of Daryl how his clients were reacting. I knew Daryl relatively well; he had been in unit one for a few years and had asked me to become a client. He didn't know that I was in the business, but I appreciated his tenacity.

I was concerned when Daryl told me that things were going well and that very few of his clients were calling him with concerns, so he figured he trained them well. Being an advisor during the dot-com bubble, the accounting scandals, 9/11, and in management during the financial crisis, European crisis and so many more world events that rocked the market taught me that communication was key. Many clients would not call when in distress. They knew that the market sometimes got very volatile and sometimes they felt embarrassed or uneasy about calling. This didn't mean that they weren't concerned or afraid, or had no questions. This was such an important time for an advisor to help guide people through the difficult times. That was when I told him the flower story.

The Flower Story

I remember when I was first married, my wife said to me, in kind of an angry tone, 'You never bring me flowers anymore.' I loved my wife and didn't understand the big deal about flowers. The next day, after work, I went to the store and bought her flowers and brought them home. 'Here, honey,' I said. 'Here are the flowers.' And I gave them to her.

"So, Daryl, how do you think that went over with her?"

Daryl curled his nose, furled his eyebrows and shook his head as if to say *you're an idiot.*

"You are right, Daryl, it did not go over very well. You see, it was not the flowers that were the issue here. It was the proactive thought, without being asked, getting off of work, getting into my car, thinking about how much I love my beautiful wife and proactively going into the flower store, buying the flowers and bringing them to her, without her asking. It's not about the flowers, it's about showing her that I am thinking about her when she is not around and knowing that I still love her and care about her."

Daryl looked like he wasn't sure where I was going with this.

"You see, Daryl, clients know that you don't control what happens in the market or control pandemics, they just want to know that you care. Similar to my wife, the flowers weren't the issue. It was the proactive thinking about her and doing something just for her so she knew I was thinking about her and that I cared. This is similar to clients. We need to proactively think about them. Even though they likely know things will work out okay, we need to pick up the phone, proactively, ask questions, and ensure they are in the right investments for them. If they are, give them the confidence and validation they need to make it through a difficult time. If they are not, take the time to understand and make the necessary adjustments."

"Being proactive has really helped my business, Cal." Daryl cleared his throat. "Most advisors think they are doing a good job if their clients don't call them, but to set myself apart, showing I care has really helped." Daryl grinned.

This discussion with Daryl reminded me of the many difficult times in the markets. During those times, fund flows turn negative, which basically means more people are selling than are buying. Fund flows tend to be negative when markets are down and tend to be positive when markets are up. This goes against the basic rule of investing—buy low, sell high. However, even today, people still tend to buy high and sell low.

One of the most delicious things about the escargot at The Keg was dipping the bread in the garlic butter left behind by the escargot. As I dunked my piece of bread into the leftover melted garlic butter and slid the delicious morsel into my mouth, I declared, "Losing weight is simple, Daryl."

Daryl had a smile on his face, looking at my figure, which was definitely more of a keg than a six-pack. I am definitely not a model for fitness. "Really, Cal? It doesn't look that way from this vantage point." He laughed.

"It's simple Daryl, but not easy. Eat less, eat healthier and exercise more . . . simple, but not easy. The reason that it is not easy is that we are emotional human beings and we tend to react on emotion rather than on logic and what we know to be true. Coming home from work after a long day, it is much easier to have something that is packaged and throw in the oven than to cook for myself. It is also much easier to turn on Netflix and binge-watch my favourite series than it is to spend thirty minutes exercising. But imagine if you had a coach, a personal trainer, who was able to stop you from overeating—eating the extra cookie—and was able to motivate you to exercise. Do you think that would work to help you lose weight?"

"Yes, likely it would. I think most movie stars have personal trainers that they see on a regular basis to help them get into shape for movies and stay in shape. What are you getting at?"

"You see, Daryl, a lot of investors try to do it themselves, like dieters try to do it themselves. Investing is simple: buy low, sell high. It's not complicated. Unfortunately, most investors don't have the knowledge, experience, self-discipline or emotional strength to do that. Money can be very emotional for people, and it can cause a lot of anxiety, especially when things are uncertain or volatile. Part of our job is to be that personal trainer for investments, talk clients down when they don't have the emotional wherewithal to stay invested, or better yet, buy more when the market is down. They are afraid and uncertain as to what is coming—every time they feel it is easier to binge-watch than to exercise, meaning every time it is easier to sell their investments, go to cash and wait until things 'get better' before going back in. Help them make the tough choice that is better for them in the long term. Eating pie feels good temporarily, but in the long term, it is bad for us and we may feel bad about it. Similarly, making poor investment decisions makes you feel good for the short term, but not the long term."

Daryl nodded in agreement.

"What you do for a living is very important, Daryl. You give advice, and lots of times advice is difficult to hear and hard to implement, but it helps your clients. In March of 2020, we saw the largest negative fund flows in history, and people were selling like crazy. Fortunately, you had the difficult conversations and took the time to care about your clients. Those that sold when the Toronto Stock Exchange was down thirty percent would have missed the very quick rebound that happened only a few weeks later. If they moved their money into GICs it would have taken them decades instead of weeks to get their money back."

I remembered giving a presentation to the managers at Mainland Financial in December 2019, just before the pandemic, and discussing the importance of giving advice. I shared the history story with them.

The History Story

Imagine we have a time machine, and you and I go back twenty years to December 1999. We meet in my office. You have $100,000 to invest and ask me where I think you should invest your money. I tell you to invest in equities. I then tell you what is going to happen over the next twenty years.

First of all, the dot-com bubble we are currently in will burst.

The darling company of the TSX, Nortel, will eventually go bankrupt.

Shortly after the dot-com collapse, 9/11 will happen and three thousand people will die in the Twin Towers.

This will trigger wars in Afghanistan and Iraq.

Then will come a major accounting scandal.

There will be a major hurricane called Katrina causing billions of dollars of damage.

There will be a major housing and financial crisis.

You will hear terms like subprime mortgage and real estate collapse.

At the end of 2010, Time magazine will call this the decade from hell.

Shortly after that, the US debt will get downgraded.

There will be a European financial crisis.

There will be something called Brexit.

Donald Trump will become president.

There will be oil spills, global warming, and uncertainty.

Then the President will get impeached.

Then, and only then, I want you to sell.

Would you invest in equities knowing that all of this would happen over that twenty-year span?

No?

Had you invested in the TSE300/TSX/S&P, you would have made over 6%.[1]

The restaurant manager came over to our table and introduced himself.

"Hi, my name is Jordan I am the manager here. I hope you are enjoying your meal today." Jordan was dressed

1 TaxTips.ca. Some of the earlier TSX/S&P composite index total return data was from Libra Investment Management Inc., sourced from the Canadian Institute of Actuaries. Data from recent years is from Yahoo Finance.

very professionally in black pants, a white shirt and black tie.

"It is terrific, as usual," I replied with a smile.

Jordan dropping by made me reminisce about the dinners my friend Kevin and I shared at The Keg.

Kevin was a good friend of mine and we meet at The Keg for dinner about every four to six weeks. I always ordered an appetizer, followed by a steak, sometimes with lobster, and we finished it off with some delicious pie. My bill was rarely less than a hundred dollars, whereas, by going out to a cheaper restaurant, I could usually get dinner for two for less than fifty dollars. However, I enjoyed my time with Kevin and loved this terrific meal with him.

Financial freedom means many different things to so many different people. My financial plans were set out ahead of me, with a good pension and regular contributions to my RRSP and TFSA, I knew I had enough for retirement. I had taken the time to run the scenarios, knew how much I needed to save and did it. I had tough years similar to what Jason Vickers or Emily Selvage had experienced. Paying myself first and having automatic transfers made the saving simple, but not easy, but over time it became easier. Because I had a good emergency fund, I was able to spend the rest of my money as I saw fit, I could spend it on whatever I wanted. I realized in that moment that financial freedom—spending $125 on a steak and lobster dinner—was not about the steak, the lobster or the delicious pie. It was my relationship with Kevin, a friendship that lasted decades. A way that the two of us could celebrate not only our decades-long friendship, but also our successes. Once again, I was learning that financial freedom has less to do with the actual money, but is about our relationships.

Taking a sip of wine, I turned my mind back to the dinner I was having with Daryl.

"I am having some ethical dilemmas, Cal," Daryl said, looking like a man going through torturous thought. "I want to help my clients and grow my business without being a salesman. I want them to deal with me, but I want to ensure I am giving good advice. People are different: some people just want a product to buy, some want advice, some listen, and some don't. How do you deal with that?"

After over fifteen years of managing financial advisors, this was the question that most of them asked. In fact, this was a question I wanted them to ask until they realized that they were asking the wrong question. The right question to ask was, "How do I ensure my clients' interests are always more important than my own?" Too often, I saw advisors with short-term goals try to sell investments or insurance to generate commission, whereas those that last in the wealth management business always put their clients' interests ahead of their own. They work for an organization that puts their customers' needs first.

"Daryl, that is a dilemma that a lot of advisors have. Their managers are pushing them to sell more, and they have to figure out what to do. What the advisor may not realize is that the manager is actually wanting the advisor to figure out what their job is. Their job is to help people, not to sell them something. They may have to see five people before one person fits their profile of a good client, and the key is to figure out, and quickly, whether or not you can help this person."

Daryl leans forward with interest.

"Being a good financial advisor is like being a doctor. Can you imagine walking into the doctor's office, sitting in the little room with the bed that has the paper on it that comes from the roll, kind of like a large roll of paper towel, and saying, 'Hey doc, I have a pain in my stomach that I am concerned about,' and imagine if the doctor turned to you and said, 'Well I have eight pills, which one would you like?' This doctor is not asking about the pain, not doing any discovering of the underlying issues, he's just trying to come to a solution without doing any diagnostics or asking any questions. I can't imagine too many doctors would last if they treated their patients this way. He would be doing nothing more than selling drugs, and on top of that he is not helping you. If this were your doctor, I would tell you it is time to find a new doctor. This is what some financial advisors do: they just go right to the solution without understanding the underlying problems, concerns or goals—just trying to sell an investment. Doing the right thing and putting the customer first means you have to do the upfront work. You must find the problem that the customer has first and only then come up with a solution. Your job is not done there. In order to truly help them, that person needs to act on your recommendation. That is where the dilemma and sales part comes in. In order to know you are doing the right thing, you must first care about the person who is sitting across from you and then believe in your solution. Unlike a doctor, whose solution, if wrong, can be very bad for you, in most cases investment solutions like GICs or balanced mutual funds will likely not hurt anyone very badly if they are not right. When a customer walks in, the question must be, 'What is this customer's problem, and how can I help them come up with a solution?' The question cannot be, 'What is this customer's problem and how can I help them come up with a solution *that I provide*?' The second question is what causes your dilemma. A good advisor knows quickly whether or not their solutions will help them and will be sure to refer them to a more suitable person that can implement the solution the customer needs. I learned over the years that if I was going long periods without being able to help people implement their solutions with me, it was because of one thing: I was focused on my needs, like selling or trying to close the deal, and not focusing on the needs of the customer. People are intuitive and they are very good at sensing how invested you are in their needs. Being a good financial advisor is a marathon, not a sprint."

"Can you give me an example?" asked Daryl.

"I was chatting with Emily Selvage the other day. We discussed a number of things, but one thing I talked to her about was her group RRSP. She was unable to access it until retirement, so it was a long-term investment. When she spoke to her boss, he suggested that she invest it in savings. Emily will not touch this money for at least thirty years, but after some discussion I suggested she talk to you and invest it more aggressively. Her boss recommended savings because he lost money in the financial crisis and in the pandemic. I think he was truly trying to help her do the right thing, but he was biased by his own experiences, where he made some bad decisions. I showed her the rule of seventy-two."

"Can you remind me what that is?" Daryl leaned forward.

"I explained to her that the rule of seventy-two requires you to take the interest rate and divide it by seventy-two. That is how long it would take for your investment to double. I walked her through what it meant. I explained the difference between investments, like GICs, that would pay closer to three percent, versus a managed fund that would likely be closer to six percent over the long term and the results came out like this." I sketched it out on one of the napkins.

Emily's Age	3%	6%
20	$4,000	$4,000
32		$8,000
44	$8,000	$16,000
56		$32,000
68	$16,000	$64,000

"Knowing what I told you about her boss's experience, why do you think that a young person like Emily would not invest her retirement savings in the investment fund?"

"Probably because of the risk?" Daryl replied.

"Yes, I would agree with that. She may not want to buy the investment fund because it is too risky and she could lose money. Let's talk about that risk. If she invested in the investment fund, how much could she potentially lose?"

"Well, theoretically, if the investment fund were to lose all of the money, she could lose everything," Daryl replied.

"That is correct," I said. "Theoretically, she could lose all of her money and instead of having $16,000 by the age of sixty-eight, she would have nothing. Now, let me ask you, what are the chances that she loses all of her money in a good-quality investment fund?"

"Not very good," Daryl said, "since all of the underlying assets would have to go bankrupt, this would likely include all of the big banks, big telecoms, oil companies, governments that have bonds in there, so, while it is theoretically possible, it is highly unlikely."

"I would agree with you. The chances of her losing the $16,000 are extremely low. Now, how much could she potentially lose by investing in the GIC?" I asked.

"What? Nothing," said Daryl. "The GIC is guaranteed."

"I disagree. The investment fund, at six percent, could grow to $64,000 versus the $16,000 that she would make in a GIC. So, she would lose the opportunity to make the difference between the $64,000 and the $16,000, which is $48,000. So, by investing in the GIC instead of the investment fund, she could potentially lose $48,000. To put it another way, by investing in the GIC, she loses the opportunity cost of the investment fund. Now, let me ask you, what is the likelihood of the investment fund earning six percent?" I asked.

"Based on historical numbers and the history story, I would say it is pretty good," he replied.

"So, if it is very unlikely that by investing in an investment fund she could lose a maximum of $16,000 and it is highly likely that by investing in a GIC she could lose $48,000, which of these is riskier for Emily?"

I could see that Daryl had never thought this way about investments before. He believed that GICs, provided they had CDIC or CUDIC coverage, were risk-free. He believed that opportunity cost was theoretical and not a true risk. I could see the lightbulb go off as he realized that if Emily made the wrong decision on her RRSP while she was young, it could cost her tremendously in retirement.

"You see," I continued, "the risk for Emily, if she were to buy the investment fund, would be like the person wanting to lose weight, not having a coach to help her stay on the right path, helping her be successful. This is where you come in. By helping Emily when times are tough and keeping her on the right path, you will be able to help her reach her retirement goals."

There is an old saying that if you do something that you love, you will never work a day in your life again. By putting the needs, and not the wants, of his customers first and believing in his solutions, Daryl's job can be made much more enjoyable. By truly caring about his customers, Daryl will not have to work a day in his life again.

Advisors getting into the wealth management business for the money instead of helping people with their goals of financial freedom will never be free themselves. True financial freedom, in this business, is not about the work. It is about the relationships and truly caring for the person sitting across from you.

Key Learnings

- Remember the flower story—in any relationship, it's not about being right, it's about how much you care.
- The risk of opportunity cost can be higher than the risk of losing money.
- Finding a good financial advisor means finding someone that puts your needs first.
- Volatility in the stock market is normal. Have a long-term strategy.
- Investing, like losing weight is simple, but not easy.

CHAPTER 7

Retirement—It's Easier Than You Think.

I poured myself a cup of coffee and made my way to the front deck of my unit. The view overlooking the lush courtyard where we hosted our barbeques with the trees and squirrels was very relaxing. Saturday mornings were a time to relax and enjoy the beautiful fall that the Okanagan provided. As I sat down, I noticed Dale Andrews coming through the gate. He must have just come back from dropping his wife Marie off at work at the grocery store. Dale had been a captain of the fire department for twenty-five years and was very involved in the fires of 2003. I couldn't imagine what he saw and experienced every day as a first responder.

"Hey Dale," I called. "Come and join me for some coffee."

As Dale made his way to my unit, I went inside and grabbed some blueberry bran muffins that I had picked up at the grocery store. I set them on the glass table and poured Dale a cup of coffee.

"You look tired, Dale, rough night?" I asked inquisitively.

"No, not really," Dale responded. "I am just ready to pack it in. The job has become a little too much. I want to retire, but I don't think I have enough money saved. Everything I read said that I need a million dollars to retire. I don't know if that is true or not, or how much I need."

"Well, maybe you and I can figure that out, Dale. I have dealt with many people looking at retirement. I have found that if you can plan and have an idea of your readiness for retirement, people tend to enjoy their last few years of work better. You see, there are three main variables when it comes to retirement. One: what age would you like to retire? Two: how much income do you need at retirement? Three: how long will you be in retirement for? Of course, the third one we have little control over, as it is basically how long are you going to live. For most of my clients, we plan to age ninety-five."

"Wow!" said Dale.

"While the average life expectancy is less than that, the fact is that for a couple aged sixty-five, there is a fifty percent chance that one of them will live to age ninety. As far as retirement age goes, that is also interesting. More and more of our clients don't actually retire at their first retirement; they just change careers. Maybe they worked in an office their whole lives and now want to work at Home Depot helping people plan for home improvement projects, or maybe they enjoy gardening and want to work in a nursery. This is an opportunity to do something that they love instead of just what they have always done. As far as income goes, that is where planning really helps. Most financial planners and books will likely tell you a percentage of salary that you want to retire on, but that is very much a guess. Let's start with when."

"Well," Dale started. "I am fifty-three now and have been with the fire department for twenty-five years. I can begin my pension at age fifty-seven, I think."

I could see the exhaustion in Dale's pale blue eyes as he recounted his age and pension options.

"Dale, as a government worker you have a defined benefits pension plan, which is a plan based on your income and years of service. You have a 'magic number' of eighty-five. This means that when your age and years of service together add up to eighty-five, you will be eligible to retire with an unreduced pension. So, in four years you will have twenty-nine years of service and will be fifty-seven years old. That adds up to eighty-six, so yes, I think that will be a good age for you to retire. In four years, Marie will be fifty-three. Do you think she will want to retire then also?"

"I think Marie will want to continue to work part time for a few more years," Dale said.

"Okay, so let's start there, Dale. Let's say you retire at age fifty-seven and Marie will continue to work for a few more years. If you have a net worth statement, a pension statement, bank statement and a copy of your and Marie's paystubs, please go get them for me. With this information, and a hand calculator, we can do what I call a quick and dirty retirement plan."

I could see Dale's shoulders begin to relax. It was obvious that this had been weighing on him for a while. As Dale walked across the grassy courtyard to his unit, I went inside and refilled my coffee. The aroma of vanilla hazelnut coffee filled the kitchen. It definitely smelled like a weekend morning.

Last year, I suggested to Dale that he keep all of his financial information on the computer and any hard copies in a binder, with originals of his will and power of attorney in his safe deposit box. Keeping everything organized and simple to retrieve relieves stress as it makes it easier to gather this information for financial planning purposes or to retrieve for the bank if someone needs a loan, mortgage or some other kind of credit.

Dale strode over with his information and set the binder on the table between us. "Here is everything I have. I have been keeping pretty good records. As you can see, I am very motivated to retire," he chuckled.

"We know when you want to retire, age fifty-seven, and we know that we want to plan a retirement until Marie's age ninety-five, so we are talking about planning for a long time, more than forty years," I said.

Dale's pension plan would allow him to retire early, and Marie would be able to retire at a young age as well. With forty years of retirement ahead of her, she would likely be retired for more years than she worked.

"Let's discuss how much income you will need in retirement. How much do you need?" I asked, knowing the answer that was coming.

"I have no damn idea," was the reply.

I chuckled. "I know, that is a tough one. Well, let's see if we can work that out. My first question is, if you had the same amount of money you have now, during retirement, do you think that would be a good starting point?"

Dale nodded emphatically. "Yes, that would be great."

My first task was to figure out how much money Dale actually lived on. Some of the advisors I have worked with would go through a budget and try and write down all of the expenses, estimating holiday gifts, car repairs, and the like. Another common way was to take a percentage of their income. Seventy-five percent was a common number to use as an estimate. My preferred way was to see how much take-home pay someone had currently, eliminate expenses that would no longer be applicable and add any new expenses in retirement. I pulled out pay stubs for Dale and Marie. They looked like this:

Item	Marie	Dale
Monthly Gross Pay	$3,333	$7,500
Monthly CPP/ EI Deduction	$236	$313
Monthly Pension	$0	$600
Monthly Union Dues	$0	$225
Monthly RRSP Contribution	$167	$0
Monthly Staff Fund	$20	$40
Monthly Income Tax	$403	$1,396
Take-Home Pay	$2,507	$4,926

After looking at these amounts, it seemed that their combined take-home pay was $7,433 per month. When I went through this with Dale, he wondered aloud, "Wow, where does all of that money go?"

"This is our starting point, Dale, let's start there. You need to earn, after tax, $7,433 per month to live the lifestyle you have now at retirement. Now let's make some adjustments."

Dale nodded. "I'm ready."

"Tell me, Dale, can you think of anything that you will no longer be required to pay for in retirement?"

Dale pondered this for a few moments. "Well," he said, "I guess we won't need to save money monthly anymore. We could likely stop our RRSP and TFSA contributions. Currently we save about $550 per month between RRSPs and TFSAs."

"Okay, that's a good start," I said. "What else?"

"Our mortgage will be paid off when I turn fifty-six, just before I retire. Oh, and Marie's car loan will be done about then as well."

"Currently, you are paying $1,150 monthly on your mortgage, and Marie's car loan is $400 per month, so there is another $1,550 monthly that you won't be paying after retirement. That brings us to a total of $2,100 per month that you are paying now that won't be necessary after retirement." I jotted it down on the pad of paper I kept by the front door.

Dale's Spousal RRSP Contribution	$300/month
Mortgage (Paid off when Dale turns 56)	$1,150/month
Marie and Dale's TFSA Contributions	$250/month
Marie's car loan	$400/month
Total expenses eliminated in 4 years:	$2,100/month

"After subtracting the savings and debt payments from your take-home pay, you are living on $5,330 per month. It is great that your mortgage will be paid off prior to retirement; you will no longer need to make that payment. I have seen some people take a mortgage into retirement and have seen others downsize to pay off their mortgage; these are very common scenarios. Since you will be retired, there is no need to pay into retirement plans anymore. If you find that you have extra money, you will likely add to your savings, but there is no reason to delay your retirement or reduce your retirement lifestyle to plan for those savings," I explained. "Now Dale, let's add some things back. What more do you want to do in retirement that you don't do now?" I asked.

I could see that Dale has given this a lot of thought as he began to speak.

"Well, we want to travel every year, Marie wants to join the book club, well it's actually more of a wine club, but they call it a book club." Dale chuckled. He continued, "I would also like to put some money aside for another car in a few years."

"Tell me about your travel plans, Dale," I said.

"We actually love it here in the Okanagan, but I have always wanted to do some travelling to the southern United States and into Central America." Dale smiled.

"How much do you think those trips would cost you?" I asked.

"Well, I think we could manage it for about $9,700 per year," Dale replied. With such a precise number, I could tell that Dale had put a lot of thought into this.

"You seem to have decent cars. What are your thoughts about that?" I asked.

"I think we will need to replace our cars in about five years or so. I think if we were able to save $20,000 every five years, I think we could manage. We are not looking at driving luxury vehicles," Dale responded.

We determined that they would like to spend $10,000 per year travelling, to save $4,000 per year towards a new car, and the "book" club dues will be $60 per month. When we added this all up, we came up with $14,720 per year, or $1,227 per month. Therefore, we needed to adjust their income needs upward by $1,227 per month. After adjusting upward, we were up to $6,560 per month. I jotted this down on the pad of paper:

Take-home pay	$7,433
Less: Expenses no longer required	-$2,100
Plus: Retirement goals	+$1,227
Total:	$6,560

"Dale, it seems that you will need $6,560 in your bank account after tax every month. In Canada, in some cases, we can split your pension income between the two of you. In your case, we are also able to split your Canada Pension Plan as well. The Old Age Security payments that you will receive at age sixty-five will be the same for both of you and when Marie turns sixty-five, you will be able to split your RRSP income, once you convert it to a RRIF. Now we have to figure out what you need after tax. The total income that you will require will be $6,560 per month, and that means that each of your incomes will need to be

$3,280 per month, or $39,360 per year. You will each be in about a twenty percent tax bracket in retirement. Since we will be able to split most of your income, you will be able to stay in a lower tax bracket. If you couldn't do that, you would likely find yourself in a higher tax bracket and your RRIF income might be closer to thirty or forty percent taxed. Your choice to set up a spousal RRSP where you are the contributor and Marie is the annuitant was a good choice. This will offer you more flexibility in retirement, as it will help to even out your income, keeping your taxes lower before and after age sixty-five. It is very important to plan for this while you are still working," I explained.

Dale laughed. "I am glad I did something right."

"All right, Dale, we know how much you need after taxes in retirement: a total of $39,360. Now we need to estimate how much you will need in total, enough to pay tax. When you retire, you will get the same tax credits you get now, but there are a couple more like the age credit and pension tax credit that you may qualify for. Knowing this, based on your twenty-percent tax bracket, a good rule of thumb is to add twenty percent to your after-tax income. This will account not only for the tax you pay but it will also take into account the tax credits you get to claim. Based on this rule of thumb, it looks like you will each require $39,360 plus twenty precent, which equals $47,232. Combined, you will require an income of $94,464." I illustrated it for him on the pad.

After-tax income required	Add 20% for taxes	Total income required
$6,560 X 12 = $78,720	$15,744	$94,464 or $47,232 each

"Wow, that is quite a bit of money that we are going to need, Calvin," Dale exclaimed.

I nodded in agreement. "We have four variables we can play with here, Dale. We can decrease your life expectancy—I wouldn't recommend that." I chuckled. "We can also decrease how much you need during retirement. In other words, reducing the vacations you decide to go on, or just spending less money. We can save more money now, or we can extend your work life. Before we do any of that, let's first see where you stand at age fifty-seven."

We pulled out Dale's pension. With twenty-nine years of service and an income of $90,000, Dale would likely receive a $52,000 per year pension. At age sixty, Dale, could begin receiving his Canada Pension of $8,900 and Marie could receive $7,200 at her age sixty. Their combined Old Age Security at age sixty-five would work out to $17,500.

"Something we need to remember," I explained to Dale, "is inflation. Every year your expenses will go up. What is nice about your pension and the government pensions is that they go up every year with inflation. This means that your pensions are indexed to inflation."

Because his pensions are indexed to inflation, I was able to show Dale his retirement based on today's dollars, as both his expenses and incomes would go up with inflation.

"Okay Dale, we have roughed how much money you need in retirement, a total of $94,464 per year, and we roughly know how much you will receive from all of your pensions. Your pensions will provide you with $85,800. It looks like we have a shortfall at retirement. Since you are retiring before you receive your CPP and OAS, you have a larger shortfall between ages 57 and 60." I wrote it down for him on the pad of paper.

	Annual	Monthly
Income Required	$94,464	$7,872
Dale's Pension Age 57	$52,200	$4,350
Combined CPP Age 60	$16,100	$1,342
Combined OAS Age 65	$17,500	$1,458
Total Income	$85,800	$7,150
Shortfall	$8,664	$622

"As you can see, Dale, when you retire at age fifty-seven, you will receive $52,200 in pension income and you would be short by $42,264 per year. In this case, you can either push back your retirement date, or you and Marie could each find some part time work to make up the shortfall. We find that a lot of people find jobs, and usually jobs that are interesting to them, when they retire young. As you enter your sixties, you can see that the shortfall will get smaller. It is closer to $26,000 at age sixty and then lower yet at age sixty-five. In case you don't want to continue working, you can push your retirement dates back, or reduce the amount of money you want to get in retirement. Another option we have is using your savings. As you can see, you have a shortfall of $8,664 at retirement. A good rule of thumb is to multiply your shortfall by twenty-five. This number assumes inflation, and also assumes drawing down on your principal. In order for you to fully retire at age sixty-five, living the lifestyle that you want, planning life expectancy to Marie's age ninety-five, you would require savings of $8,664 times twenty-five, which equals $216,600."

Dale looked shocked.

"Since you don't have that much money, I would suggest that you both keep working for a couple more years, or part time. When you retire at age fifty-seven, you can begin drawing on your pension, therefore the shortfall at your age fifty-seven will be $42,264. Since Marie currently earns that much, if she continues working you will be fine, or you can both semi-retire and each of you would only need to earn $21,132 or about $1,761 per month each. Some people like to work part time, others like to work full-time but seasonally, say at the golf course or at the nursery. At age sixty, you can begin drawing on your Canada Pension Plan. However, you will still have a shortfall at age sixty. Because you will be receiving about $17,500 in OAS, your shortfall will reduce from $42,264 down to about $24,764 per year. Now you will have some more choices to make. You can continue to work until age sixty-five, or you can start to draw on your savings," I continued.

Dale nodded, looking thoughtful.

"Let's see what we would need for both of you to retire at your age, fifty-seven. You won't be receiving CPP until age sixty and OAS until age sixty-five. In this case, because it is short term, my rule of thumb is to multiply $42,264 time three years, which equals $126,792. We can make up the shortfall between ages fifty-seven and sixty by having $126,792 in the bank. Now let's talk about the shortfall between age sixty and sixty-five. At age sixty, you will be receiving your work pension along with your CPP. This totals $68,300, which means you have a shortfall of your $94,464 retirement need and the $68,300 you will be receiving, which is a total of $26,164. Again, for simplicity we will need five times that amount, or a total of $130,820. To recap this, Dale, here is what you will need for both of you to retire at your age fifty-seven." I wrote it all on the pad of paper and handed it to him.

Age	Amount Required
57-60	$126,792
60-65	$130,820
65+	$216,600
Total Savings Required	$474,202

"Most bank websites will have calculators that we can use to calculate the present value, which means the amount you need today, using differing rates of return and different time frames. So, let's break down each calculation. You are currently fifty-three, therefore, for number one, we need $126,792 by age fifty-seven, which is four years from now. For number two, we need $130,820 at your age sixty, which is in seven years. For number three, we need $216,600 by the time you turn sixty-five, which is in twelve years. We have three different time horizons, therefore we will use three different interest rates in order to ensure the time horizon matches the risk level we are willing to take. For number one, we will use 2% since it is a safe GIC rate. For number two, we will use 4%, allowing for some equities. For number three we will use 6%."

Again, I drew it out for him on the pad of paper.

Years invested	Amount required	Interest rate	Amount required
4	$126,792	2%	$117,136
7	$130,820	4%	$99,412
12	$216,600	6%	$107,643
Total	$474,212		$324,191

"You need roughly $324,191 today in the bank, to retire fully at age fifty-seven. How much do you have saved?" I asked.

"We only have $90,000 saved," Dale responded despondently.

"All is not lost, Dale. As you can see above, your biggest cost is the amount between age fifty-seven and sixty. What if you both continued to work part time until you turn sixty-two? This would do a number of things. It would eliminate the need for number one altogether. It would reduce the need for number two, as well. It would also increase your CPP income because you would defer it to age sixty-two."

Dale looked impressed.

"Now things change quite a bit. First of all, the shortfall between age fifty-seven and sixty is still there, at $42,264 per year. Between the two of you, do you think that you could make up this shortfall with different work?"

"Yes, I think so," replied Dale. "Marie actually likes her job, she could go part time. I have always wanted to work at the golf course, plus I would get free golf." Dale grinned.

"Okay," I said, "great! Let's redo our calculations based on that."

	Annual	Monthly
Income Required	$94,464	$7,872
Dale's Pension Age 57	$52,200	$4,350
Combined CPP Age 62	$20,424	$1,702
Combined OAS Age 65	$17,500	$1,458
Total Income	$90,124	$7,510
Shortfall	$4,340	$362

"Here is where we stand now. At age sixty-two, you require $94,464. You will have $52,200 from your pension and $20,424 from CPP, for a total of $72,624. This means you are short $21,840. At age sixty-five, you will have a total income of $90,124 and will be short $4,360 per year. Breaking it down again, here is what you need." I turned to a fresh sheet of paper.

1. $20,424 for three years
   age sixty-two to sixty-five
   =$61,272

2. $4,360 X 25 = $109,000

"Your total has now been reduced to $170,272. Let's do the same calculation as we did before." I jotted it down for him again.

Years invested	Amount required	Interest rate	Amount required today
9	$61,272	4%	$43,048
12	$109,000	6%	$54,170
Total	$170,212		$97,218

"As you can see, the amount required today is $97,218. With the $90,000 that you already have saved and by continuing to save your $300 spousal RRSP and your $250 TFSA contributions every month until you retire from the fire department at age fifty-seven, it works out to $6,600 per year and will be close to $20,000 by the time you are fifty-seven. By no means, Dale, is this a fulsome retirement plan, but it does show that you can retire from the fire department at age fifty-seven. By changing your paradigm a little bit, you are able to make retirement achievable. I would suggest that you take that lovely bride of yours out for dinner and talk about what retirement looks like for you and explore the trade-offs of retiring early and some of your retirement goals. You can discuss each of your retirement ages, whether you work part time or whether you actually need all of that money in retirement."

"Wow, thank you, Calvin! I know this is not a full plan, but this 'rule of thumb' quick and dirty way of calculating retirement really helps us to set some realistic goals. This really helps Marie and I begin a discussion."

As Dale, with a bit of a skip in his step, walked home, I realized that financial freedom wasn't necessarily about having all the money. It was about living with hope. So many people I ran into didn't take the time to calculate what their retirement income would be or what it would look like. It seemed that Dale would be able to relax a bit. With a goal that was achievable in his mind, he could now have freedom to enjoy his job more, living and loving pre-retirement with his wife. It seemed financial freedom for Dale wasn't about having millions of dollars. Instead, it was the ability to relax and have hope.

Key Learnings

- When setting retirement income goals, take your current take-home pay and take off what will no longer spend and add any new retirement expenses.
- Retirement doesn't need to mean stop working, it may mean doing something different.
- Take time to plan, and dream, about retirement.
- By spending time calculating retirement income, it may be more achievable than you think.

CHAPTER 8

Leave a Good Family Legacy with Estate Planning

"Nice shot, Mr. Bennett," Emily Selvage said as she gave me a high five.

The grass courtyard in the middle of the Lakes was the perfect place to play Saturday afternoon bocce. It was a beautiful day and being friends with my neighbours really made living at the Lakes great.

This week, I was partnered with Emily Selvage, playing against her parents Brett and Kelly Selvage. Brett was one of the nicest guys you would ever meet. Kelly was a very pretty forty-one-year-old woman. She had Emily at a relatively young age. She dressed very well and kept her hair and nails perfect. I imagined she liked to keep herself looking her best while she was selling all of those diamonds and gold bracelets at the jewellery store in the mall.

"I don't know if you heard, but I just received an inheritance last month, Cal," Kelly started. "I wondered if we could pick your brain for some advice?"

"Sure." I rolled the green ball up close to the small white ball, which I learned earlier that day was called the pallina. "What can I help you with?"

"Well," Kelly glanced over to Brett, "we are going to pay our credit cards and car loan off with our inheritance and then use the rest to pay down our mortgage."

"That sounds like a pretty good plan," I replied.

"We think so, too," Kelly continued, "but now that we have all of our debts paid off and Emily will likely be moving out soon, Brett and I can't decide what to do with the life insurance that we have. It is important for us to ensure that we leave some money for Emily and our future grandkids, but we are paying $100 per month on this life insurance policy. Now that our debts are paid, and Emily will likely move out in the next couple of years, we don't think we need it anymore, but we have had it for twenty years. We bought it when we were very young and have been paying into it for many years."

"Tell me about the policy," I said.

"Well, it was a universal life policy. We have heard that term insurance is cheaper, but given our age at the time, we bought Brett a permanent life policy for $500,000 and I had one for $250,000. It seems like such a waste to get rid of it now. We have some cash built up in it and we can take it, or we can continue to pay the premium and, I guess, one day Emily will get the money."

"I find it interesting when young people purchase permanent life insurance," I began. "It can be quite a bit more expensive than term insurance; however, there are some cash benefits, and also it can help with retirement planning and estate planning as well. Sometimes people just go for the cheaper option, but with insurance, as with most things in life, you get what you pay for." I turned to Brett. "Can you tell me about your retirement plan at work, Brett?"

The barrel-chested forty-three-year-old picked up the red ball with his big arms. "I have been working as a heavy equipment operator for a road maintenance company for the past fifteen years, and in that time, I have built up a pretty good defined contribution pension plan. I think it's a good plan, but I am not sure, really."

"Well, Brett," I replied, "this type of pension means that you and your employer each contribute every paycheque to this pension, but instead of the pension income being based on your income and years of service, like a defined benefits plan, you must choose where the money will be invested. At retirement, you can choose to move the pension into a Life Income Fund, also known as a LIF, which would remain in the investments that you choose and you will draw an income from it. There is a maximum withdrawal amount in your sixties somewhere around 6-7% per year that you will be able to take monthly, or you can purchase a life annuity that will guarantee an income for life. The nice thing about the LIF is that if you pass away, the balance of the LIF will end up going to your beneficiary, in this case Kelly, and when Kelly passes away, the balance will be paid out to her beneficiary, likely Emily. The concerning thing about the LIF is that the income is not guaranteed and is dependent on the investment performance. The nice thing about the life annuity is that the income will be guaranteed for life. However, when you pass away, if it is a joint life annuity, some or all of the payments will continue to Kelly, but when Kelly passes away, the annuity dies and Emily won't get anything. Choosing pension options is very important, as it will have major implications on your retirement income. It is quite complicated and people should get help when making this choice. Too many people try to make the choice alone without getting advice."

Many people, including me, were intimidated by Brett, with his large chest and arms. His bald head and salt and pepper goatee made him look meaner than he actually was.

"I don't like going to people for advice," Brett said. "I don't trust people."

"Let me give you an example of the type of advice you can get from talking to someone. Have you guys heard of a concept called pension maximization?" I asked.

"Does that mean contributing the most I can to my pension?" Brett replied.

"No," I said. "It means getting the maximum income out of your pension. Let's discuss how annuities work."

Brett and Kelly glanced at each other. Kelly nodded in agreement.

"When you retire, Brett, you may want to have a guaranteed pension. Assuming you retire at age sixty-five, you could get a pension that goes for the rest of your life. Through your defined contribution plan, you can purchase a pension, which is called a life annuity. A life annuity pays out an income for your life. Brett, your life expectancy will be about eighteen years at age sixty-five, meaning on average a man your age will live to age eighty-three. Kelly, on the other hand, will be only sixty-three at that time, and generally, women live longer than men. Her life expectancy will be age eighty-five, or twenty-two years. When you go shopping for a pension, you will have a few choices to make. First of all, you can get an annuity on only your life, which means that you will receive a pension for as long as you live, but when you die, the pension dies with you."

"The pension would just end?" Brett asked.

I shook my head and replied, "Usually there are guarantee periods of five, ten, or fifteen years, which means that if the person receiving the pension, called the annuitant, dies, the payments will continue to the beneficiaries for the guarantee period. The second choice is you can get an annuity that pays for your life and for Kelly's life. The problem with this is that the annuity is issued by an insurance company that will work with actuarial tables based on life expectancy. If you get a life annuity on only your life, as a sixty-five-year-old male, the insurance company will estimate that they will pay out for eighteen years. However, if it is a joint annuity, they will be adding a sixty-three-year-old female. Now instead of paying out for only eighteen years, they will likely be paying out the pension for twenty-two years, which is 22% longer than just for you. Given that the insurance company would have to pay out 22% longer, it will likely result in a lower payout on a joint annuity; since the amount in the defined contribution plan will be a specified amount, the annuity option will be higher or lower, depending on which pension you choose. There are many variations on this. For example, there is an option that, instead of Kelly getting the same pension after you die, you could choose for her to get 60% of the pension that you receive. Since the insurance company would pay out less after you die, Brett, they would be able to give you a higher pension amount when you retire and then it would drop to pay Kelly 60% of what you received when you pass away."

Emily was not impressed with this conversation, since my concentration and focus had shifted to financial planning.

"This is so boring," she complained.

Kelly gives her the look that mothers give their kids when they are annoyed by them. She pulled out one of her business cards and a pen out of her purse and I drew out what Brett's pension options might be on the back of the business card.

Option	Pension	Brett	If Brett dies, Kelly receives
A	Single Life Annuity	$3,500	$0
B	Joint Life Annuity	$2,730	$2,730
C	Joint Life 60%	$3,100	$1,860

"Kelly," I started, "There are basically three options to your pension as you can see. To be fair, there are usually multiple options with different guarantee periods, inflation adjustments and beneficiary amounts ranging from 50% to 80%, but this is the basic idea. Option A means that Brett will receive $3,500 per month for his whole life; however, when he dies, you will receive nothing. Option B means that Brett will receive $2,730 per month, and when he dies, you will receive the same $2,730. Option C means that Brett will receive $3,100 per month, but when he dies, you will receive only $1,860 per month."

Emily scowled, as my next throw wasn't even close to the pallina.

I turned back to Kelly. "All right, Kelly, which of these options, A, B, or C, will you choose for Brett?"

They both laughed, and Kelly said, "Option B, of course, because I want to ensure I am able to take care of things when and if Brett dies before me."

"That's good thinking, Kelly, but the problem is the pension will only pay out $2,730 instead of the full $3,500, which could hinder your retirement plans."

Brett chimed in, "But this is how pensions work, and I want to make sure Kelly is taken care of."

"Of course," I said. "That is important when it comes to your retirement with Kelly, but let me ask Kelly a question." I turned back to Kelly. "In order for you to collect your $2,730, what would have to happen to Brett?"

Kelly replied, "Well, he would have to die."

Brett's eyes widen as he ponders his own mortality.

"Yes," I replied. "You are correct. Brett would have to die. So the option you are choosing is that you both would give up $770 per month as a retirement pension so that in the event that Brett dies, you are taken care of, and have income for life. Does that sound right?"

"Yes, I guess you are right," Kelly replied skeptically.

"So," I said inquisitively, "what do we call a product that we pay money for so that in the event that one person dies, the other person will be taken care of financially?"

"Life insurance!" Brett burst out.

"Yes, Brett, you are right. This is why people buy life insurance. So that in the event that a breadwinner dies, the other person or people are taken care of." I continued, "In this case, you guys would be giving up $770 per month so that in the event that Brett dies first, Kelly would get $2,730 income per month. Also remember that the $2,730 pension she receives after Brett dies is taxable and Kelly will have to pay tax on it. Let me ask you guys another question. In the event that Kelly dies first, do you think the insurance company will bump the pension back up to $3,500?"

"I doubt it," Kelly replied.

"I doubt it too," I agreed. "What if, instead of choosing option B, you choose option A. What if, also, you kept the $500,000 of universal life insurance? You would be able to receive $770 extra per month, and in the event that Brett died first, Kelly could then either draw an income from the insurance, or if she didn't need the income, put in the bank. She could invest the $500,000 and take her income from that or otherwise, purchase her own life annuity. Since the life insurance is tax free, there would be much less tax to pay on the income, so she wouldn't need as much to draw an after-tax income. Also, in the event that Kelly died first, Brett can simply change the beneficiary to Emily and when Brett passes away, Emily would collect the $500,000 cheque."

"Oh yeah!" Emily yelled. "That is the choice you should make! Mr. Bennett, you are the best bocce partner ever!"

Everyone laughed.

"I guess we should keep the life insurance, hey babe?" Brett said.

Kelly nodded.

"I really appreciate the advice," Brett said. "I usually don't go to people for advice, I tend not to trust them."

"Before implementing a plan like this, it is important to get advice on your specific situation from a qualified professional. But, yes, I agree, keep the insurance to give you more options at retirement," I replied.

"I have been in the advice business a long time," I added, "and I have found that women tend to seek out advice more than men. That includes asking for directions."

Everyone laughed, except for Kelly.

"Sorry, everyone," Kelly said. "I'm just thinking about when Mom passed. I wish she would have got some advice before she died."

"I know the estate process can be difficult. Not only is it emotional, but there are lots of legal and governmental issues to deal with. How did all that go for you?" I asked, knowing that dealing with an estate can sometimes be a painful experience for people.

"Oh my gosh, it was terrible," Kelly said. "My older brothers were the executors on my mom's estate. It took over a year for us to get any money because there were legal fees and taxes. My oldest brother, Greg, got Mom's RRSP and my other brother, Terry, and I got the proceeds from the house. Well, as it turns out, Greg got the cheque for the RRSP, but the taxes came out of the estate, which was our portion, so Greg ended up getting more than Terry and me at the end. Also, Greg got his money right away and Terry and I had to wait over a year. On top of that, our lawyer said that Greg may be entitled to even more money because he wasn't mentioned in the will because of something called the will's variation act. Greg was allowed to take out executor fees, so he and Terry took what they could, which worked out to 5% of the estate. Now, with Terry and Greg fighting over executor fees and Greg getting way more than us and talking about the will's variation act, nobody is talking to each other and there is a big fight going on. My mom would be so upset if she were alive to see what has happened." Tears welled up in Kelly's eyes.

"What can someone do to make it easier?" Brett asked.

"Estate planning can be a very complicated subject," I started. "There are a few things that someone should think about. First of all, naming family members as executors may save money, but it is a headache. Often, people think they are bestowing an honour on someone by naming them as executor, when in real life, it can be a real headache. Not only can it be complicated, but there are legal responsibilities, and being the executor, beneficiaries will be looking to you for answers. Many of our clients choose to hire a professional executor. Let me give you a few ideas to think about. First of all, most of the executor fees, the legal fees and probate costs are caused by the money in the estate. When someone dies, certain assets can bypass the estate and be paid out directly to the beneficiaries if the asset allows for beneficiaries. Here are some examples of plans that may allow someone to name a beneficiary and bypass the estate."

Kelly passed me another business card, and I wrote this down on it:

- Any registered plans like RRSP, RRIF or LIF
- Tax-Free Savings Accounts
- Products purchased through an insurance company liked GICs, savings accounts or segregated funds
- Life insurance

Kelly and Brett peered over my shoulder as I wrote.

I cleared my throat. "Something else that bypasses the estate and all of the fees that go along with probating an estate are joint accounts with the right of survivorship. This means that if, for example, a savings account is shared jointly with another person, when the first person dies, the account will transfer directly to the joint holder without going through the estate. This can be helpful for married couples and other simple situations. However, it can cause some legal and tax problems, so anyone doing this should consult their accountant or lawyer first. Essentially, whatever you can have with a named beneficiary will help to bypass the estate, allowing the funds to go directly to the beneficiary without all of the legal, probate, and executor fees and without going through the probate process. One thing to be careful about, as you and your brothers experienced, is that if you only name one beneficiary on your registered plans, they will receive the proceeds of the RRSP or RRIF plan."

Kelly nodded glumly.

"However, the tax will most likely be charged to the estate, leaving less money in the estate. Sometimes it will use all of the money in the estate, and in that instance the beneficiary would need to pay some or all of the tax. By giving the beneficiaries equal share in the assets that have named beneficiaries as well as equal share in the estate, there is a better chance that the deceased's wishes will be met."

"Oh, I see." Kelly reached for Brett's hand.

"Any assets that are not in plans with named beneficiaries or are not joint with right of survivorship will go to the estate. The estate is governed by a document called a will. So, by naming beneficiaries, in most cases, the will does not govern those assets. The person or people who oversee the will are called an executor or executrix. If you have a simple estate and do a really good job of estate planning, you will have most of your assets fall outside of the will and move quickly into the hands of the beneficiaries. For most people, visiting an estate planning specialist can help with more complex issues. Here are a few things your mom could have done to make things easier."

Kelly passed me a third business card, and I wrote down the following:

1. Name all three kids as beneficiaries on her RRSP
2. Name all three kids equally in the will
3. Ensure her non-registered assets, as much as possible, were in a Tax-Free Savings Account naming the kids as beneficiaries
4. Put the balance of the non-registered funds into insurance GICs or segregated funds
5. Hire a professional executor

"There are likely a number of other things that your mom could have done to save on fees and taxes, but most of all, heartache for you and your brothers," I said.

Kelly started to tear up again. "I really wish I would have known those things before. This has really torn our family apart."

"OMG!" Emily yelled, putting an arm around her mom and giving her a squeeze. "Enough talk about death! Let's play bocce, I need to win something."

We all agreed. Kelly picked up her ball and aimed at the pallina.

I found it interesting that had Kelly's mom known what happened upon her death, her view of financial freedom would have been shattered. In my experience, financial freedom, for a lot of older adults, was having the comfort that their money can bring joy to their families and bring their families closer. Unfortunately, all too often the money that was left could tear a family apart rather than bring them together. Proper estate planning could do good for a family, whereas poor estate planning can have a lot of unintended consequences.

Key Learnings

- Life insurance can be used to help improve your pension.
- Use investments with named beneficiaries as much as possible.
- Ensure your estate plans bring your family together—not tear them apart.
- Take time to understand your pension options.

CHAPTER 9
The Barbeque

My mother has two famous dishes that she makes: turkey soup and potato salad. For the annual Lakes Barbeque, I felt that making the potato salad was the better choice.

As I exited my unit and made my way into the centre courtyard, I saw that Dale Andrews and Jason Vickers were manning the barbeque. Everyone knew they cooked the burgers and hot dogs, whereas the real work of bringing all of the food out and setting up the picnic table and all of the fixin's was done by Jessica Walters, Marie Andrews and Kelly Selvage. I set the potato salad on the table and reached down into the ice-filled cooler to grab a cold Corona.

I pulled my folding lawn chair up next to Daryl Jagger, who was sitting on a chair with the word Canucks written across the back with the old orange and black skate logo.

"It's been a great year, Cal," Daryl started. "Thanks for your help."

I smiled at Daryl. He was one of the good ones. Focusing on how he could help the bank customers not only achieve their goals but find out what their goals were had helped him become the trusted and successful advisor that he set out to be.

"Do you like to travel, Daryl?" I asked.

"Yes, I love it," he replied.

"Financial planning is very similar to planning a trip," I said. "One of my favourite things in the world to do is to travel. I have spent hours planning trips and I always start my planning asking myself where do I want to go. Some of my favourite places I have been include that little village in Tuscany called Fonterutoli, having coffee with the locals in Nicosia, Cyprus, and touring the wineries in my hometown. Planning for travel is very similar to financial planning. You need to plan where you want to go, how you are going to get there, when you want to go and what you want to do when you get there."

Daryl nodded. "That makes sense, Cal."

"When I plan a trip, I always start with the question 'What do I want to do?' That usually leads into the question 'Where do I want to go?' After that, I have to find hotels and figure out how I am going to get there. The trip to Tuscany was difficult because I had to fly into Rome. After that, I caught a train to Florence and there, I rented a car to get to my place in Fonterutoli. It was complicated! Without speaking Italian nor understanding Italian, dealing with some of the road signs, toll booths and which places to trust was a challenge."

"It sure sounds like it!" said Daryl.

"But there is one main difference, in my experience, between financial planning and trip planning. For most people I meet, when they plan a trip, the destination and time frame of when you are going comes first. When it comes to financial planning, I find most people start with the how they are going to get there instead of the where and when are they going. Should I buy mutual funds or stocks? Should I invest in ETFs with low fees as a do-it-yourself investor? How much should I put away every month? Some advisors, the salesman type, start here as well. However, like planning a trip, it is best to start with a destination in mind. There are four steps to setting goals. It doesn't matter if you are deep in debt or have millions of dollars, the steps are the same."

"Actually, that is right, Cal, it is like planning a trip," Daryl said. "Tell me about the four steps."

"Here are the four steps, Daryl." I ticked them off on my fingers for him. "First, list three things you want to achieve. Examples of this would be: I want to go to Italy, I want a new hot tub, I want to retire, I want to pay off my credit card, or I want to put my child through university. You can have four, maybe five at the most. The problem is that if you have too many goals, your resources will be spread too thin and you will not achieve them. If you only have one goal, then your priorities will be compromised, you may overlook enjoying life today or, conversely, not planning for your future."

Daryl nodded along with me.

"Secondly, after you have listed these three items, prioritize them. Rank them from one to three, with number one being your most important goal and number three being the least important. Prioritization is important because you may have to start with very little resources and focus on just one for the short term before you can go onto priorities two and three in the longer term."

"I see," murmured Daryl.

"Thirdly, now that you have three prioritized goals, next you want to make them time-bound. When do you want these things to happen? Examples might be that you want to retire at age sixty, or go to Italy next spring, or your child might start school at age eighteen, which is fourteen years from now. Like planning a trip, sometimes the time frame may vary. Maybe flights are too expensive at that time, maybe hotels are sold out due to a specific event. Some items, like education, can be fixed. This would be like planning a trip where you are going to see the tulip festival in Washington State. The tulips will not wait for you. You will want to have at least a general idea of when you want to go."

Daryl took a drink of his beer. "What's the fourth step?"

"Now you have three prioritized, time-bound goals, next you will want to quantify those goals. How much money are we talking about, roughly? The trip to Italy will cost $10,000. I want to retire with the same money I am making today. Education costs will be $20,000 per year, that new hot tub will cost $6,000. You will not likely know the exact cost, but by putting a dollar amount beside it, you make it real."

"So," said Daryl, "Is it like when you plan a trip, and you ballpark hotel costs, car rentals, and flights?"

"Exactly." I nodded. "With these four steps completed, it is now that we can make these goals realized. For planning a trip, we will start to search out hotels, flights and car rentals, and whether your timing is right, or even if the destination is right. Similar to financial planning, by using a financial planner or using online tools, you can research what the costs are and do the planning to reach these goals. Additionally, if there are two of you, it will be important that you agree on your goals; otherwise you will be travelling to two different places. The first step in any journey, whether it is a financial journey through life or a journey across the world, is to find out where you want to go. As a financial advisor, I have found satisfaction from my work by helping people, and there are some very basic things I can do to help. The first thing is goal setting."

"Oh boy," Daryl said. "I too often start with asking about risk or comfort with the market. I really need to start my advice by helping people with goal setting. Maybe I can call myself a financial travel agent," he laughed.

I smiled as I saw Emily Selvage emerge from unit seven with some hot dog and hamburger buns. I knew she would miss these barbeques with these "old" people when she eventually moved out into her new place.

"Daryl helped me learn about something called dollar cost averaging," she said as she approached.

I was glad that she was able to meet with Daryl and get her group RRSP sorted out.

She continued. "He explained that by buying regularly, I limit the risk I am taking and can earn a good return on my investments. Since I am investing every month, I don't have to have it build up in my savings and invest once per year, I can just invest small amounts every month and then not worry about it, kind of like set it and forget it. After that, I meet my advisor once a year for a review of my goals and to see if I am saving the right amount of money."

"Tell me more about that, Cal," Brett Selvage said, wandering over.

"This concept is helpful to the average investor who is saving on a regular basis. Essentially, it is investing regardless of what is happening in the stock market, since timing the market is very difficult. For the person utilizing a dollar cost averaging strategy, who is in it for the long term, a declining market is their friend, but so is a rising market, good all around. For example, if you invest in a mutual fund every month and the market continues to rise, you will make money because the units you purchase every month will rise with the market. If the investor invests every month and the market goes down and then up (which is what the Dow Jones and TSX have done all through history), they will also make money. This is because as the market declines, they buy more units and if you have a long-term time horizon, the market will eventually rise again, and you will make money. This same strategy can lose money over the long term if the investor invests in only one or two stocks. That is risky because those one or two stocks could go to zero without any real effect on the stock market as a whole. If an investor invests in a broad-based mutual fund, they will likely only lose money long term only when the market goes down and stays down. To date, this has never happened, but if it did, I suspect we would have other problems than the investor losing money. For example, let's look at two different investors, Dick and Jane. Dick invests $100 per month for six months in a rising market and Jane invests the same amount for six months in an up and down market. Let's see how they do."

Brett looks interested.

I pulled a napkin out of my back pocket. "Here is Dick's $100 per month investment into a mutual fund. Each monthly investment will purchase a specific number of units of the mutual fund, they will accumulate until after month six, where he will sell at that price. In Dick's example the price went straight up over time."

Month	January	February	March
Investment	$100	$100	$100
Price	$5	$6	$7
Units purchased	20	16.7	14.3

Month	April	May	June	
Investment	$100	$100	$100	Total
Price	$8	$9	$10	$10
Units purchased	12.5	11.1	10	84.6

"In this example, in January, Dick invested $100, and the share price was $5 per unit. He picked up twenty units. In February, Dick invested another $100 and the price has risen to $6 per unit; this time he picks up 16.7 units. This can be calculated by dividing the $100 investment by the unit price, in this case $6. This continues on for the next six months. Dick invested a total of $600, his units went up to $10 each and he purchased 84.6 units. His total investment has risen to $846, which is a pretty good return. He invested $600 and now has $846 for a total return of 41%."

"Wow!" said Emily, who was still listening.

"In Jane's example, she invests $100 per month but instead of going straight up, we see a market that goes down and up."

I turned the napkin over and wrote on the back.

Month	January	February	March
Investment	$100	$100	$100
Price	$5	$4	$3
Units	20	25	33.3

Month	April	May	June	
Investment	$100	$100	$100	Total
Price	$4	$5	$6	$6
Units	25	20	16.7	140

"Jane has invested a total of $600, but the investment price rose very little from start to finish. The unit price was $5 in January and finished at $6 in June. This was much different than Dick's investment, which started at $5 in January and ended at $10 in June. However, Jane has accumulated one hundred and forty units over the same time period. At a value of $6, this gives her $840, virtually the same amount as Dick; however, she was investing in a volatile market. She benefitted when the market went down and was able to pick up more units. When I am talking to young people, I will often show both dollar cost averaging and the rule of seventy-two, as these two simple concepts can help them achieve their longer-term goals."

"That's interesting," Brett replied. "Does this work for older people like me as well?"

"Actually, Brett, you are already doing it," I explained. "Because you have a defined contribution pension plan, you and your employer are investing every two weeks into your pension, which is going into a managed investment portfolio and utilizing the dollar cost averaging strategy."

"Cool," Brett replied, puffing out his chest like a peacock showing off his beautiful feathers.

I smiled over at Emily. I suspected there was a good future client for Daryl there. She was well on her way to a good financial life.

"Hey Cal," yelled Jason Vickers, "do you want cheese on your burger?"

"No cheese, thanks," I replied. It was great to see Jason change his perspective on financial freedom from the accumulation of things to a more inward focus. We have all heard that happiness does not come from things, but from relationships, and it comes from the inside, not externally. Financial wellness starts in the same way. By using our financial means to build relationships and share experiences with those we love, rather than trying to build up things to impress those that we don't really care about, we can change how we view financial success. Maybe the greatest things in life are free, but those things that we used to try increasing our ego, like impressing others, are very expensive.

Over the past few months, I had seen a change in Jason. After selling the truck, the stress level went down. Instead of trying to impress the "hot girls," he saw the true value of his own self-worth and met a girl who liked him for who he was. She shared the goal of buying a house with Jason.

"Hey Marie," Dale Andrews called, "Bring out the champagne."

All heads turn to unit two as Marie Andrews walked out with a bottle of Dom Perignon.

"What is this about?" asked Kaylin Williamson.

"March 19, 2020," Dale said emphatically, while giving me a wink.

March 19, 2020

On the evening of March 18, Dale and I were on his deck drinking our favourite winter drink: Baileys and coffee. His investments were getting hammered as COVID-19 was entering North America with a vengeance and the TSX, which had been at 17,970, had dropped to 11,721, a drop of almost 35% in less than a month. He was distraught and upset. He wanted to sell his investments.

"If you sold, what would you do with the money?" I asked.

"I would put it on the sidelines until we knew the full extent of the virus," he replied.

The United States and Canada were in the midst of shutting everything down, and Dale was convinced we were going to see depression-like unemployment and didn't know where the bottom was.

I slowly took a drink of my coffee and said to him, "This virus is temporary until we get a vaccine. How long do you think it will take to get back up to where it started: 17,970 on the TSX?"

Dale's response was the same response I got from my advisors during the financial crisis in early 2009. "Oh my god, it could take three or four years before it comes back."

"Well, Dale, let's assume you are wrong, and it actually takes five years to come back."

Dale looked like he was going to cry. "Do you really think it will take that long?" he asked.

"Dale, I have no idea how long this will take, but let's assume five years. If that is the case, then the TSX will have to rise by the same 6,249 points that it fell to go back from 11,721 up to 17,970 where it started. That would mean the TSX would have to rise 53% during that period. This is a longer-term case than you had feared. Rising 53% over that period would mean a compounded rate of return of about 9%. If you move your money, where else are you going to make 9% today?"

Dale looked very confused after this comment. He explained that things felt terrible, we didn't know when this was going to end, and just felt he needed to get out.

"Our economy is very resilient," I started to tell him. "We have been through the Great Depression, World War 2, the Cold War, 9/11, the financial crisis, and just last year we set record highs in the stock market. This, too, will pass. If you sell now in order to make more money, you will have to invest during a time that you feel worse than you do now. Everyone will feel worse if the market goes down further. For most investors the best thing to do is to keep your money invested and ride through it. Often during times like this, we see some of the largest negative swings in the stock market, but we also see some of the largest positive swings as well. By selling after a few very negative swings, you will likely miss out on some of the largest swings as well."

"Okay, Calvin," said Dale. "I will take your advice and not do anything rash. There is the matter of the $12,000 that I have sitting in a savings account right now. What should I do with it?" He asked.

"Well," I said, "It is very difficult to time the market, but I do remember in 2002 and 2009 there were some similar opportunities to this. When I look back on those opportunities, I wished I would have invested when the markets were down. I would suggest buying into this market. I am not sure how long you will be in it for, or how low it will go, but buying low is half of the battle." Dale ended up putting the $12,000 in and ended up making 25% on his money quite quickly when he sold two months later, in early May.

Marie brought over the Dom Perignon. Kelly put out the plastic champagne glasses. As Dale poured, he explained to us that when he gets a windfall, he likes to take 10% of whatever it is and share it with the people he loves. This Dom represented 10% of the gain he made on the $12,000 investment.

Over the years, helping the average investor, I have seen emotions cloud their judgment when it comes to investing. I have seen people fall in love with stocks or mutual funds that go up and not want to sell and, more often, seen people exit their investments when the market goes down. This was normally due to a lack of knowledge or information. People forgot that when they sold they were crystallizing their loss. They had a lack of faith in the investment they had. They didn't realize that, in order to make money selling in a down market, they had to buy in when they felt worse and the market was even lower. If they were selling because they felt bad, it was highly unlikely they would invest when the market fell even more.

On the other hand, there were those that thought they could time the market and get out, thinking things were so bad that they will get back in when it goes down. In my experience, those investors missed the bottom, kept waiting for the bottom to happen, and completely missed it. They ended up getting in when the market was much higher. Either way, selling high-quality investments in a down market as part of a long-term strategy just didn't work. As far as Dale Andrews's idea of sharing 10% of windfalls with the people he loves goes, I thought it was a great idea.

Everyone lifted up their glasses and yelled "Cheers!" except for Henry Walters, who yelled "Moo! Moo!"

All faces turned to Henry, and Jessica just laughed. Henry was referencing the Cow and Milk Story.

A few months ago, Henry and I were chatting about his TFSA. He wanted to know how to invest in equities with some of his longer-term investments using the Calvin Bennett method. I told him the Cow and Milk Story.

The Cow and Milk Story

Investing for income is like buying dairy cows. We are buying the cows for the milk. The milk in this case is dividends, and the cows are the underlying stocks. Buying high-quality dividend-paying stocks that pay a regular, rising dividend, with a good history of paying dividends, is a great way to get a regular income. What we care about is the milk production, and hopefully increasing milk production. When we produce this milk, we can buy more cows.

The price of beef will go up and down, but we don't really care about this as long as milk production stays the same. In fact, we like it when the price of beef goes down, because then we can by even more cows with our milk. Sometimes there is a huge run up in beef, and then we may consider selling some of our cows, but because of the milk production, we don't need to sell our cows. We need to be careful, because sometimes a virus can temporarily reduce the amount of milk that is produced or a cow might get sick and reduce production, but overall, as a long-term income strategy, buy cows for the milk.

One thing I have learned about investing for dividends over the years is that with high-quality dividend-paying stocks, the investment community will keep the stocks higher because the dividend yield rises when the stock goes down. For example, if a high-quality bank stock was trading at $100 and was paying a $4 dividend annually, this would result in a 4% dividend yield. The $4 dividend divided by the $100 stock price would be 4%. When the entire market drops quickly, as it did in 2008/2009 and in 2020, the dividend remains the same, but the price of the stock drops. Maybe the stock drops 40% to $60, but still pays the same $4 dividend. This would result in a 6.67% dividend yield. $4 divided by the $60 stock price. Income investors will realize that the yield is very good and will generally start buying and earning a good income. This will keep the stock from plummeting like a stock that doesn't pay a dividend is apt to do during these times. The one thing to be careful about is if the company pays out more in dividends than profits, they will likely end up either reducing the dividend or killing the stock. Make sure that you are buying healthy cows that have proven long-term milk production.

"Hey Henry, maybe this will help you milk your cows!" Dale Andrews walked out of his unit carrying two stools that looked like they were homemade.

"Wow," Jessica replied. "Those look very nice. Did you make those?"

"You bet he did," responded Marie. "He has taken up woodwork ever since he had that retirement discussion with Calvin and chatting with Daryl."

I looked over at Daryl with a look that said *what does woodwork have to do with retirement?*

"That's right," Dale said. "I have read a quote that said *do something you love, and you will never work another day in your life*. After my discussion with Calvin, I began to think about what I want to do when I retire. I have always loved woodwork and would love to make things for people. After speaking with Daryl, he gave me a piece of advice. Why don't you tell them, Daryl?"

"I told Dale that when you retire, you want to retire *to* something, not *from* something. Too many times people retire from their job, and then, having nothing to do, no purpose, they end up getting sick and dying younger than they should. For the past forty years, they found their purpose in their jobs and now they lack purpose, so they just watch TV or do other activities that have no real purpose. I told Dale to think about what he wants to do. I asked Dale to begin a hobby and think about his next transition. I asked him, 'What are you going to retire to?'" said Daryl.

"That's right," replied Dale. "I have decided that I will retire to loving my wife, playing golf and doing woodwork. I can go my whole life doing these three things."

I remembered taking some of my retirement courses. The instructors really emphasized the point of having your clients retire *to* something and not retire *from* something. I thought I knew why. Retiring from something was the end, whereas retiring to something offered a new beginning. It didn't mean a job, but more of a purpose. It could be a hobby, volunteering, learning something new, or travel. Whatever it is, have something to look forward to.

As I looked around at the group enjoying themselves at the barbeque, I thought of the simple concepts that have helped them.

Budgeting for business is good, for personal is hard. *Pay yourself first* is a good rule to help you stay out of debt. It's hard at first, but stick with it, and you will create a great habit.

If you are looking to save for your first house, pretend you already live there, stretch yourself and save like you were paying a mortgage, property taxes, and other house expenses. Remember, your money isn't gone, it's just in another place.

When setting up your RRIF for retirement, consider the Calvin Bennett method to help get good returns and keep your investments from being depleted in down markets by being forced to sell every month.

Dollar cost averaging and the rule of seventy-two are simple ways to see how money grows and a way to save money safely and effectively. These two concepts can help people, especially younger people, save money safely and reach their goals more easily.

The role of insurance is so important in our lives. Remembering the money machine and movie theatre stories can put things in perspective.

Knowing that you get what you pay for and planning long term with insurance. Buying permanent insurance or buying term and converting some every year, can help with your pension through pension maximization or can help with giving to charities or reducing taxes.

Goal setting is key. Sometimes it is hard, but just doing it gets you on the right path. Prioritized, time-bound, quantified, realized goals are the place to start. Using the take-home pay method to set retirement goals can help with some quick and dirty calculations that can begin the process.

Investing is emotionally taxing. Like trying to lose weight, it's simple but hard. Remember the history story and the Cow and Milk Story, and also remember that when the market drops, it offers great opportunity.

Estate planning, if not done well, can wreak havoc on family dynamics. Take the time to do it right. You can't take it with you, so ensure what you have left behind makes people's lives better, not worse.

Years of financial planning experience helped me to learn a few things as an advisor. Remember the flower story? It's not about the flowers, it's about the proactive thought of showing someone that you care.

I can't be all things to all people, but I can say yes to all people. If they were not a right fit for the practice I was trying to build, I made sure I referred them to someone who could help. Even simple pieces of good advice made a difference in people's lives. As an advisor, I could help everyone, maybe not directly, but if I truly cared about them, I could direct them to a place that would give them the attention they deserved and help them achieve their goals.

As a financial advisor, even if I made the best financial plan in the world with the greatest recommendations, if people didn't do anything then I actually haven't helped them. The most important step in the financial planning process must be implementation. Without that, all we have is a fabulous document sitting on the shelf. Part of our job, like a good weight loss coach, was to not only show people how to become financially healthier but to help them actually do it. Good advice comes with action. Good advice with inaction is a tragedy.

I reflected on my discussion with Ed the bartender at the Dancing Otter. Financial freedom started with good values. I had been the dumbest smart guy around. I was focused on the number in my bank account. My goal was the fancy car. I wanted a big house. I realized financial freedom had nothing to do with any of these things. Financial freedom is how I use my money to enhance the relationships with those I care about. These could include a nice house and a nice car, but for me, I learned that financial freedom was rooted in love. Loving my family, loving myself and loving those around me. Money was just the tool to get me there. As I reflect on my life, I had financial freedom all along, but I just didn't see it. I was focused on what I had rather than who I had it with and why I had it. Reflecting on my values, I may not have owned the biggest house, or the nicest car. But I am doing something I love, I have a wonderful family, great neighbours and friends who love me. I kept chasing financial freedom, but like a certain girl from Kansas, I was there all the time. I just needed to believe it.

Key Learnings

- Financial planning is like planning for a trip—I need to know where I am going before I can figure out how to get there.
- Dollar cost averaging is a great way to save long term.
- If the market drops 33%, there is an opportunity to make 50% when it goes back up.
- The price of beef may go up and down, but buy cows for the milk.
- Share 10% of your windfalls with those you care about.
- Implement your financial plan. The greatest financial plan in the world is not helpful if you don't do something.
- Retire *to* something, not *from* something.
- Financial freedom is not about the money—it's how you use the money.

About the Author

Rod Rieu is a Certified Financial Planner (CFP®) and a Fellow of the Canadian Securities Institute (FCSI) and has been in wealth management for over twenty-six years. For twelve years he worked as an advisor but has spent the last fourteen years managing financial advisors. He enjoys helping people understand everyday financial problems and hopes his book will help them find a way to help themselves.

Rod grew up in Port Coquitlam and now lives in West Kelowna, B.C.